TABLE OF CONTENTS

Page

TABLE OF CONTENTS..

ILLUSTRATIONS ....

CHAPTER 1 INTRODUCTION 1

    The History of Ideas 1
    Grassroots Rebellion 3
    Literature and Source Review... 8

CHAPTER 2 A PEOPLE APART..12

    A New People and a New Faith... 12
    The Politics of Faith 16
    From Ulster to the Backcountry.. 19
    A People Apart 26

CHAPTER 3 BREAKING THE BACKCOUNTRY 28

CHAPTER 4 THE PAXTON BOYS 44

    At Wit's End 44
    The Massacre of the Conestoga 51
    The Paxton Boys March on Philadelphia 53
    Motivations of the March 58

CHAPTER 5 THE SOUTH CAROLINA REGULATORS 65

    Chaos in the Backcountry 65
    The Regulation 72
    Motivating the Regulation 82

CHAPTER 6 THE NORTH CAROLINA REGULATORS...89

    Arbitrary Tyranny 89
    Relief, by Peaceful Means 97
    Rising Resentment 100

    Right to Rebellion 105
    Motivating the Regulation 113

CHAPTER 7 THE VIGILANTES GO TO WAR 122

    The Paxton "Patriots" 123
    Civil War Among the Regulators 127
    Exodus to Patriotism 132
    Strain of Violence 136

CHAPTER 8 CONCLUSION 138

BIBLIOGRAPHY 143

ILLUSTRATIONS

Page

Figure 1. Map of Pennsylvania 1763, with selected settlements depicted. 45

Figure 2. Map of South Carolina 1767, before the Regulation 66

Figure 3. Map of South Carolina 1770, after the Regulation 81

Figure 4. Map of North Carolina in 1765, with select backcountry counties depicted 97

CHAPTER 1

INTRODUCTION

We look at the present through a rear-view mirror. We march backwards into the future.[1]

— Marshall McLuhan, *The Medium is the Message*

The History of Ideas

More than most other conflicts in American history, the American Revolution has captured the imagination of students and historians alike, and has provided the inspiration for a considerable library of popular history and entertainment. Doubtless this is because of the central role the conflict played in defining the American identity. Those features of the American identity that most Americans hold most dear were on center stage in this formative conflict. Modern ideologies and continuously changing historiography have provided no shortage of new interpretations on the causes, course, and outcomes of the war. But the American Revolution involved far more than the War for Independence from England. John Adams, among many others of the time, discussed the true meaning of the term American Revolution. In his 1818 letter to Hezekiah Niles, Adams was concerned with differentiating the Revolution from the war.

> The Revolution was effected before the war commenced. The Revolution was in the minds and hearts of the people; a change in their religious sentiments of their duties and obligations. . . This radical change in the principles, opinions, sentiments, and affections of the people, was the real American Revolution.[2]

---

[1]Marshall McLuhan, Quentin Fiore, and Jerome Agel, *The Medium Is the Message* (New York: Bantam Books, 1967), 74-75.

[2]Bernard Bailyn, *The Ideological Origins of the American Revolution* (Cambridge, MA: Belknap Press of Harvard University Press, 1967), 160.

While Adams' quote only scratches the surface of understanding the ideological origins of the movement known as the American Revolution, what is most interesting for the field of military history is the simple realization that revolutions tend to be organic responses to a complex set of causes all occurring within a socio-cultural context. It is, unfortunately, an all too frequent practice of undergraduate and high-school history textbooks to distill the causes of all wars to their immediate political genesis in favor of covering generals, battles, and how the war fits neatly into a narrative of an ever improving human condition. If we are, as Marshall McLuhan has suggested, marching backwards into the future, then the primary value of military history is in understanding the rich complexity of the causes of conflicts. Adams' understanding about the origins of the Revolution makes no mention of the Stamp Act or the Boston Massacre. If his assertion is to be believed, then the most complex causes of revolutionary warfare reside in the minds of the people who fight them.

Adams' generation of revolutionaries was far from being a monolithic group, unanimously engaged in a struggle for independence. Although most Americans felt that the British government had become oppressive of their liberties, not all were in support of open rebellion and independence. Many simply desired to return to "their old channel," longing to regain freedoms, as Englishmen, that they felt were lost. Others, who may have assumed that these freedoms were too far gone, could not fathom what an independent America would be like, or were too economically vested in England to consider complete independence.[3] Even the Sons of Liberty, so associated with American independence, frequently professed their faithfulness to King George. Many were

---

[3]Ibid., 141-143.

convinced that the King was the rightful sovereign, but was being misled by those "whose interest it is to represent all things to [him] in false lights."[4] Others like Thomas Jefferson, John Adams, and his second cousin Samuel were guided by a strong Whig ideological heritage. They had their minds fixed on independence long before their peers.[5] Provided the complexity and number of converging ideologies that resulted in the American Revolution, it is not within the scope of this thesis to examine each of the components, but rather to take one of the ideological lines and examine a portion of it in depth.

Grassroots Rebellion

While individuals hold ideas, understanding the motivations of individuals who lived over 200 years ago can be a daunting, if not impossible task. Even with considerable writings and a solid understanding of the events of the individual's lifetime, one can only hope to make an informed assumption about the individual's motivations. The process can feel like attempting to describe a room to someone, having only looked through the keyhole. Slightly easier than unearthing the motivations of individuals is determining the collective motivations of cultures. While individuals are certainly not defined by their culture, it would be foolish to ignore the powerful influence cultural

---

[4]Pauline Maier, *From Resistance to Revolution* (New York: Knopf, 1972), 104-105.

[5]Luigi Bassani, *Liberty, State and Union: The Political Theory of Thomas Jefferson* (Macon, GA: Mercer University Press, 2010), 22-23; The Whig theory of history was based on the belief that early Anglo-Saxons lived ideal lives in which they elected their Kings and had a great deal of authority over their own future, and that the Norman invaders brought with them the evils of hereditary and oppressive monarchy. In many ways the theory was the ideological descendant of John Locke.

beliefs, morals, and customs can have on the individual. Thus, by examining both the individual and the culture, the viewport into the room expands beyond the keyhole to something slightly larger.

The American colonies were, from their very beginnings, a culturally diverse group. Each colony exhibited a distinct character, defined by the cultures that inhabited it. Even though people from very different cultural groups often lived within close proximity, they maintained their own cultural identities well into the early beginnings of the United States. Frequently, cultural differences caused reactions of repulsion such as William Byrd II's response to working with backcountry North Carolinians during his 1728 surveying of the dividing line between Virginia and North Carolina. Byrd was astonished to find that the predominantly Baptist backcountry Carolinians did not baptize their children, and he feared, therefore, that they would "remain Infidels all their lives."[6] He held contempt for the backcountry men, referring to them as "Goths and Vandals," and purposefully attempted to exclude them from land ownership in his later Carolina land ventures.[7] His reactions to these men in the backcountry were likely driven, to some extent, by cultural biases well established in the old world. As an Englishman, Byrd would have had an inherently negative response to these backcountry men since they descended from Northern Irish immigrants. Pre-existing cultural relationships provided

---

[6]William Byrd and William K. Boyd, *William Byrd's Histories of the Dividing Line Betwixt Virginia and North Carolina* (Raleigh: North Carolina Historical Commission, 1929), 102.

[7]Leslie Philyaw, *Virginia's Western Visions: Political and Cultural Expansion on an Early American Frontier* (Knoxville: University of Tennessee Press, 2004), 22.

the frame in which much of the British North American settlement took place, and likely provided further motivation for each culture group to remain largely insular.

Among the most insular of groups to settle in the American colonies were the Scots-Irish, an almost tribal culture that immigrated in large numbers between 1710 and the commencement of the war for independence. For reasons that are further explored in Chapter 2, the Scots-Irish settled outside of the well-established port cities, frequently living in close proximity to, or on, Indian lands. Long-term migration patterns sustained this separation of cultures to such a degree that by the beginning of the war for independence, the backcountry inhabitants of South Carolina, North Carolina, Virginia and Pennsylvania had more in common with each other than any had with their coastal counterparts.[8] The power base of all colonies at the time centered on major economic hubs along the coast, dominated by Englishmen and an assortment of other minority cultures motivated predominantly by economic trade. Years of separation between the coastal elite and the backcountry yeomen created sometimes irreconcilable political, economic, and cultural differences.[9]

In the politically active decade that led up to the American Revolution, these backcountry Scots-Irish occasionally railed against what they perceived were either oppressive and tyrannical, or criminally negligent colonial governments. While frequently non-violent, at times these resistance movements broke out into open violence. Given their expressions of radical Whig thought, and the temporal proximity to the

---

[8] Colin Woodard, *American Nations: A History of the Eleven Rival Regional Cultures of North America* (New York: Viking, 2011), 101-102.

[9] Ibid.

outbreak of war, it is easy to understand why several historians have attempted to discern any ideological linkage between these backcountry rebellions and the larger American Revolution as understood by Adams. In particular, this work will examine the Paxton Boys insurrection of 1764 in Pennsylvania, and the Regulator movements of North and South Carolina.

Interpretations of these events, and of the subsequent revolution, have changed throughout history as historiography and political landscapes continuously evolve. The first recognition of the vigilantes' potential revolutionary connections came from John Hill Wheeler, who in 1851 wrote that the Battle of Alamance, in which the North Carolina Regulators were defeated by North Carolinian Militia,[10] was "the first blood spilled in these United States, in resistance to exactions of English rulers, and oppressions by the English government."[11] In claiming this, he made the first known link between one of these backcountry movements and the overall American Revolution. Others have concluded that if not explicitly ideologically linked, the defiance of these backcountry rebels may have provided an example to the early Patriots.[12] Recent scholarship seems to attempt to distance the backcountry movements from the American Revolution.

---

[10]The Battle of Alamance (16 May 1771) was a major engagement between predominantly Scots-Irish rebels in the North Carolina backcountry who called themselves 'Regulators', and Governor William Tryon's colonial militia. The battle was a major loss for the Regulators and marked the end of the rebellion.

[11]George Adams, "The Carolina Regulators: A Note on Changing Interpretations," *The North Carolina Historical Review* 49, no. 4 (October 1972): 346-347; John Hill Wheeler, *Historical Sketches of North Carolina, from 1584 to 1851* (1851; repr., Baltimore: Regional Publishing Company, 2 volumes, 1964), 59.

[12]Ibid., 347.

Historians like Robert Lambert focus on the local nature of the grievances that gave rise to these movements. In relation to the Regulators of South Carolina, Lambert wrote,

> to know the identity of certain Regulators offers little help in accounting for the backcountry Revolutionary allegiance, for the two questions are essentially unrelated. Whether or not one was a Regulator depended on how one's family and neighbors fared at the hands of the outlaws in the 1760s; but whether or not a backcountryman was a rebel in the Revolution might hinge on a number of factors, but primarily on the person's perception of the dangers and opportunities to come from renouncing allegiance to the Crown.[13]

In some ways, to claim that backcountry vigilante movements were caused by individual local grievances is similar to distilling the causes of entire wars to a few political missteps. While local grievances were undoubtedly the proximate causes of the unrest, tension between frontier cultures and the urban coastal cultures created a dysfunctional social environment in which the local grievances could occur. Additionally, Lambert lumps the entire collection of ideologies and motivations that lead up to the American Revolution in with those who desired independence from the Crown. While this was certainly the result of the Revolution, it cannot be said that this was always the goal of the Revolutionary generation.

The backcountry Scots-Irish vigilante movements of the decade leading up to the American Revolution were clearly ideologically linked to the later revolution. These links are not limited to the most proximate motivations like taxation, representation, and corruption, but extend to the more nuanced ideologies like the understanding of the role of the government, and the role of those who are governed. Whig ideological tradition played well into the cultural and religious ideals of the Scots-Irish, and the long conflict

---

[13]Robert Lambert, *South Carolina Loyalists in the American Revolution* (Columbia, SC: University of South Carolina Press, 1987), 27-28.

riddled history of the Scots-Irish made them predisposed to extralegal violence. In the end, the simple Scots-Irish farmers who settled the colonial backcountry found themselves several years ahead of the revolutionaries.

Literature and Source Review

In seeking to gain a better understanding of the myriad of ideological movements that culminated in the revolution, two works, written only a few years apart stand out from the rest. Bernard Bailyn's *The Ideological Origins of the American Revolution* was an invaluable survey of all the seemingly unrelated, yet convergent ideological ancestors of the revolution. Also Pauline Maier's *From Resistance to Revolution* was of great help in understanding the role of vigilantism in the years leading up to the Revolution. Narrative histories of the American Revolution were helpful in putting both the ideologies, and the actions of the vigilantes into the larger context of the independence movement. While narrative accounts of the conflict are vast in number, Benson Bobrick's *Angel in the Whirlwind* and John E. Ferling's *Almost a Miracle* do justice in providing an adequate understanding of the ideological, political, and military struggle that is collectively known as the American Revolution.

This thesis being partially a cultural study, a number of works provided an understanding of the Scots-Irish and the land they inhabited. Understanding the people and their place is critical in comprehending the origins of the vigilante movements, and their connections with the Revolution. James Webb's *Born Fighting* and Karen McCarthy's *The Other Irish* were valuable in gaining insight into how the Scots-Irish became the clannish warrior culture that defined a large part of the later American identity. Fully understanding the Scots-Irish backcountry men would be difficult without also gaining a broad understanding of the radical Protestant theologies that drove their worldviews. Although George Hunston Williams' *The Radical Reformation* is the premier scholarly work on radical Protestantism, Rod Gragg's *Forged in Faith* is a much shorter work focused solely on the influence of Protestantism on the revolutionary ideals. The writings of Charles Woodmason, compiled by Richard J. Hooker in *The Carolina Backcountry on the Eve of the Revolution,* cannot be omitted if one hopes to ever fully understand the complex relationships between faiths and cultures in the colonial backcountry. Not only was Charles Woodmason a contemporary of the vigilantes discussed in this thesis, he was intimately familiar with the people who comprised the Regulator movements, and even supplied his literary skill in crafting the South Carolina Regulator *Remonstrance*.

In attempting to understand the tumultuous environment the Scots-Irish coped with after they came to the American Colonies, three books guided this thesis. Mathew C. Ward's *Breaking the Backcountry*, and Fred Anderson's *Crucible of War* convincingly argue that the French and Indian War produced the unsettled backcountry environment ripe for violence in the 1760s. Eric Hindraker and Peter Mancall's *At the Edge of Empire* provide a general context for how colonists settled the colonial backcountry.

Works dedicated to understanding the vigilante movements in question are few in number compared to those covering the American Revolution, but a few works of significant scholarship were invaluable in understanding both the activities and motivations of these groups. For the Paxton Boys, Jack Brubaker's *Massacre of the Conestogas* and Kevin Kenny's *Peaceable Kingdom Lost* are short but thorough narratives of both the slaughter of innocent Indians and the subsequent march on

Philadelphia. Of the two, Kenny's book provides the better context in which to understand the insurrection.

The South Carolina Regulation is the least written about, but perhaps the most interesting vigilante movement. Richard Maxwell Brown's *The South Carolina Regulators* is the only book-length treatment of the event, but it would be difficult to surpass this thoroughly researched work. Rachel N. Klein's *Unification of a Slave State* tackles the creation of the Planter class within the South Carolina backcountry, and covers the Regulation in two chapters, but she relies heavily on Brown's research.

The North Carolina Regulation is a more popular cult topic for historians of Colonial North Carolina, but that only served to make secondary source research more difficult. Among the several works on the topic, two stand out as most worth reading. Marjoline Kars' *Breaking Loose Together* is an invaluable look into not just the Regulation but also the people responsible for it. She analyzes the factors leading to the Regulation into three discernable lines: politics, economics, and faith. She also discusses at some length the potential ideological linkages between the Regulation and the Revolution. Carole Watterson Troxler's *Farming Dissenters* is dense at times, and readers may struggle with the organization of the book, but her work brings light into areas that Kars' book only discusses in passing. Of particular interest is the section on the role of Herman Husband, and Governor Tryon's alliance with the backcountry Presbyterians.

Several sources were used in an effort to track the backcountry vigilantes of the 1760s into the mid 1770s. In order to determine whether the ideological linkage of their earlier movements guided their decisions on allegiance in the later rebellion, primary source documents were of the utmost help. The Revolutionary War Pensions records in the National Archives proved invaluable in identifying a large number of vigilantes turned Patriots. In order to avoid falsely connecting pension records with vigilantes, the records were cross-referenced by location and for the names of other vigilantes. The South Carolina State Archives and History website contains a searchable database of large numbers of digitized wills, land records, and letters which were useful in identifying Regulators as Patriots or Loyalists.

CHAPTER 2

A PEOPLE APART

In order to understand the activities, motivations and behaviors of the Scots-Irish in the prerevolutionary backcountry, it is necessary to understand the origins of the Scots-Irish people. These people are known throughout history by various names, including: Ulster-Scots, Ulster-Irish, Irish Protestants, Northern Irish, and Scotch-Irish. Patrick Griffin referred to them as "The People With No Name" in his 2001 book of the same name. Generally, the modern practice among writers on this topic is to refer to these people as Ulster-Scots prior to their immigration to the Colonies and Scots-Irish after their arrival. For simplicity and clarity, they will be referred to as Scots-Irish throughout this work.

A New People and a New Faith

The Scots-Irish culture evolved over the course of hundreds of years, shaped by several massive migrations and a profound religious conversion. The first major migration started in roughly AD 122 as the Romans built the famous Hadrian's Wall at the northernmost extent of their empire in England. While the Romans built the wall to protect themselves from the violent and untamable Pictish tribes of Alba to their north, the Dál Riata were departing the north of Ireland with dreams of domination. The Dál Riata was a collection of some of the most aggressive and warlike tribes that then occupied Northern Ireland. These raiders crossed the Irish Sea and commenced a 700-year conquest of the Picts of Alba. Although the Dál Riata gained dominance over the Picts by about AD 500, the indigenous tribe continued as a thorn in their side until a final grand rebellion in AD 834.[14] After subduing the Picts in their final display of defiance, the Kings of the Dál Riata faced another, potentially more dangerous opponent, the Vikings. Drawn together by a mutual enemy, the Dál Riata and the Pictish cultures merged through a series of royal intermarriages. King Kenneth MacAlpin married a Pictish princess, and his sons continued the practices of intermarriage between Pictish and Irish royalty, setting the stage for a wide-scale integration of these native Irish peoples with the Picts.[15] Generations of intermarriage between these two groups created a distinct new culture that was neither fully Pictish nor fully Irish.

These new people were known as the Scots, after the Roman name for Ireland, Scotia. Although some have described the early Scots as savage barbarians, they were no strangers to the refining influence of Christianity. By the time MacAlpin subdued the Picts, Scottish Christianity had existed for some 300 years.[16] From the beginning, this new brand of Christianity showed signs of distinction from the Christianity of Rome. Scottish Christians chose not to adhere as strictly to rules of Church hierarchy as their Roman brethren.[17] A millennium after missionaries first introduced Christianity to the Scots, an unconventional preacher by the name of John Knox planted seeds of dissent which later grew into the independent Presbyterianism so associated with the Scots-

---

[14]Karen McCarthy, *The Other Irish: Scots-Irish Rascals That Made America* (New York: Sterling, 2011), 5.

[15]Simon Taylor and Marjorie Ogilvie Anderson, *Kings, Clerics, and Chronicles in Scotland, 500-1297* (Dublin, Ireland: Four Courts Press, 2000), 66-68.

[16]Justo González, *Story of Christianity: The Early Church to the Present Day* (Peabody, MA: Prince Press, 2010), 236.

[17]Ibid.

Irish.[18] Knox preached a message that resonated strongly within the hearts of his Scottish congregations. In reaction to his perception of immoral royal leadership, his message was of the supremacy of the individual conscience as an authority on religious life. This divorced the individual's religious life from the control of appointed church leaders who were all too often simply wealthy members of the gentry who sought titles and positions of authority. The resulting Reformed Church of Scotland, founded by Knox and his followers, allowed congregations to elect their ministers and threw out the Anglican Book of Common Prayer in favor of liturgy of the Church of Scotland.[19] This new form of Christianity, which evolved into Presbyterianism, gave the Scots ecclesiastical license to indulge their already well-developed sense of personal independence. The move to non-state controlled clergy is a clear example of an early predilection towards independence. Other aspects of the Church's organization and theology made for a faith attractive to the independent minded. The Church of Scotland, unlike the Church of England, contained a very small hierarchical structure of church executives, with no individual head of the church corresponding to the Anglicans' Archbishop of Canterbury. While the early Presbyterians did have positions similar to Bishops, the highest level of

---

[18]McCarthy, 14.

[19]Gonzales, 83; The Book of Common Order, used by the Reformed Church of Scotland differed very little from the Anglican Book of Common Prayer with a few notable exceptions. The confession of faith in Knox's Common Order showed clear signs of Geneva's influence on him as it several times refers to the salvation of the elect.

the Church, the General Synod, was decidedly democratic. The Calvinist[20] theology of these Scots-Irish Presbyterians also likely influenced their independent-mindedness. While the Catholic and Anglican theologies placed a great deal of importance on the collective salvation of the Church body, Calvinism focused solely on the individual nature of being one of the elect.

The second major migration that contributed to the cultural identity of the Scots-Irish was what became known as the Plantation of Ulster.[21] Shortly after King James VI of Scotland took the crown of England as James I, he sought to capitalize on the gains of the Nine Years War.[22] In order to cement these gains and pave the way for further conquest of Ireland, James I began a systematic process of re-peopling Ulster.[23] He revoked the titles of Irish landholders and handed their lands over to prominent English and Scottish lords. Few of these nobles had plans of transplanting from their comfortable estates and starting anew in the north of Ireland. Instead, they used their new land as an

---

[20]Martin Luther saw salvation as a result of faith, which required the free will to either accept or reject Christ. John Calvin, on the other hand, felt that mankind was completely incapable of influencing its own salvation. This understanding naturally led to God being seen as not just arbiter of salvation, but also the determiner of who was to receive grace. This led to the Church, and faith itself being seen as not required for salvation. Faith and church membership were thus seen as evidence of salvation, rather than the process of salvation.

[21]In the context of the time, the word plantation referred to an organized colonization. The etymology is linked directly to the horticultural sense of the word. Colonists were 'planted' abroad and multiplied.

[22]The Nine Years War in Ireland (1594-1603) was unrelated to the much larger Nine Years War of 1688-1697. The war of 1594-1603 was fought between the most powerful Irish clans and the expanding English rule in the island. England expanded from the lands just around Dublin to seizing most of Ulster.

[23]Pádraig Lenihan, *Consolidating Conquest: Ireland 1603-1727* (Harlow: Longman, 2008), 18-23.

economic venture, offering long-term leases to poor Scots and Englishmen. In order to improve the appeal of living in conflict-torn Ulster, they offered leases in terms of generations rather than years.[24] Thus moving a family from Scotland to Ulster offered the potential of a generational improvement of the family's lot. The Plantation of Ulster also offered James I the ability to remedy another nagging problem, that of an exceptionally violent group of Scots living along the border of Scotland and England, people known as the Border Reivers. After hundreds of years of conflict between the two countries, the area along this border deteriorated into a lawless land where people fended for themselves. Bandits roamed the countryside, forcing the inhabitants to patrol the lands and enforce their own laws as they saw fit. In the years prior to the reign of James I, the monarchs of Scotland felt indifferent towards this situation. Once James I essentially unified the crowns of England and Scotland, the Border Reivers became a problem that needed to be addressed. James' answer was to send them to Ulster. This simultaneously solved the problem of establishing control over the border region, and helped populate Ulster with a people quite used to fending for themselves in lawless lands.[25]

The Politics of Faith

The first few years of the plantation likely convinced the Scots-Irish that they had finally arrived. They were able to support their families by farming sizeable tracts of land. They worked the land in groups of a few interrelated families, sharing the duties

---

[24]Tyler Blethen and Curtis Wood. *From Ulster to Carolina: The Migration of the Scotch-Irish to Southwestern North Carolina* (Raleigh: North Carolina Department of Cultural Resources, Division of Archives and History, 1998), 16-20.

[25]Andrew Himes, *The Sword of the Lord: The Roots of Fundamentalism in an American Family* (Seattle, WA: Chiara Press, 2011), 21-22.

across all their lands, often times farming the land to exhaustion. Once their lands were no longer productive, they simply left their allotted lands in favor of other lands still unsettled.[26] This made administering the plantation difficult for the English royalty and naturally aggravated the already slighted Irish Catholics, who were forcefully displaced from their own lands. The evidence of their response to the invasion of the Scots-Irish is apparent in the architecture of surviving buildings of the plantation era. Each small community had a strong house, or fortification, which provided safety for the neighboring families in case of attack by the Irish. One of the surviving Presbyterian churches of the time had gun ports in strategic locations just large enough to fit a musket through.

The religious environment was contentious not only between Presbyterians and Catholics. Many English settlers decided to take the generous land offerings in Ulster as well, bringing with them their Anglican faith. The precarious balance of faiths in the north of Ireland was tipped to one side or the other at various points early in the plantation. Shortly after the English Civil War and the execution of Charles I, Oliver Cromwell sent forces into Ireland in an attempt to subdue the entire island. While the main goal was to subdue the Irish Catholics, Cromwell's forces killed many English and Scots-Irish Protestants as well.[27] Cromwell's forces brought with them more than just death and destruction; they brought with them a faith even more radical than Presbyterianism. The army brought the faith of the Baptists. While the Presbyterians were fiercely independent and distrustful of any state-controlled church hierarchy, the Baptists

---

[26]Blethen and Curtis, 9-10.

[27]Ibid., 5.

took this to a new level. They believed that each church was a religious institution in and of itself, not beholden to any central authority.

After Charles II re-established the English monarchy, the balance of faith in Ulster was once again upset. Charles II continued Cromwell's suppression of the Irish Catholics, establishing a series of rules known as the Penal Laws, which kept the Catholics from serving in any position of power, leaving the administration of the land solely to the Protestants.[28] This change in balance would pale in comparison with the ascendency of James II to the crown. King James II, the brother of Charles II was unapologetically Catholic, having spent a great deal of time living in France after the execution of his father. King Charles II sought to mitigate the problem of James' religion by forcing him to sign a promise that he would raise his children Mary and Anne as Protestants.[29] James agreed and raised his daughters as Protestants; however, after his first (Protestant) wife died, he remarried, to a Catholic. Under James' logic, the agreement that he made with Charles II only applied to children of his first wife, and thus he raised the son of his second wife as a Catholic. As a male, James II's Catholic son, also named James, would become heir ahead of James II's older Protestant daughters. Massive political upheaval resulted almost immediately from the birth of this new heir to the throne. The resulting Glorious (or "Bloodless") Revolution not only deposed James II but further forged the fighting spirit in the Scots-Irish cultural identity.

---

[28] W. C. Taylor and William Sampson, *History of Ireland* (New York: J. and J. Harper, 1833), 223-224.

[29] Maureen Waller, *Ungrateful Daughters* (London: Hodder and Stoughton, 2002), 92.

After James' Protestant nephew, William of Orange, quickly defeated King James II in England, James fled to Ireland in hopes of building a large all-Catholic Army. While he recruited this army, he directed that all garrisons in Ulster strongholds be replaced with loyal Catholics. While he was successful in re-manning the garrisons of several strongholds, as his forces approached the town of Londonderry, a number of youths stole the keys to the city gates and locked the town up. Several months later, in April 1689, James II marched his loyal Catholic army on the city and demanded that they open the gates.[30] The Scots-Irish response was to open fire on the ousted King and his guards. The Catholic army laid siege to the city and it appeared as if James II would get his way. Disease ran rampant throughout the city, and many accounts tell of sporadic cases of cannibalism as supplies ran out. For 105 days, the defenders of the city of Londonderry fought off hunger, disease, and the forces of James II, who traded cannon shot and insults with the town's inhabitants. In late July, naval forces of William of Orange broke through large barriers along the river Foyle and ended the siege. James II's army headed south, where they were defeated at the Battle of the Boyne almost a year later.

From Ulster to the Backcountry

Despite their victory over James II and the firm reassertion of Protestantism as the religion of the realm, life for the Scots-Irish did not significantly improve. William's reign was cut short after he died in a riding accident. His sister-in-law, Anne took over and began a systematic process of alienating the Scots-Irish of Northern Ireland. Anne

---

[30]Patrick Arthur Macrory, *The Siege of Derry* (Oxford: Oxford University Press, 1988), 304; James' army was not big enough, nor did they have enough heavy artillery to launch a large scale assault on gates or city walls.

was a strong Anglican, seeing England as not just a Protestant kingdom, but more specifically an Anglican one.[31] The Penal Laws, originally established under James I to suppress the political involvement of the Catholics, quickly expanded to all non-Anglicans in Ireland. These expanded laws prohibited non-Anglicans from any political involvement, excluded them from a number of prominent universities, and invalidated their marriages unless overseen by an Anglican priest. In many cases, members of dissenting faiths had to pay a tithe to the Anglican Church of Ireland and their clergy had to swear to say state prayers for the monarchy at each meeting.

Although these policies of religious oppression on the part of the British crown undoubtedly created significant motivation for the Scots-Irish to leave Ulster, most sought opportunities elsewhere due to economic frustrations.[32] The overwhelming majority of Scots-Irishmen in Ulster did not own the land they worked. They still benefitted from the three-generation leases their great-grandparents signed during the initial plantation. By the early-mid eighteenth-century, most of those leases were coming due for renegotiation. Much to the surprise of the renters, the prices had increased significantly. Families that had farmed the same land for over 100 years found themselves forced to move to smaller plots of land, or in some cases, lost their land entirely. In addition to the problem of lost land, those who had managed to retain their lands found that they were not able to turn their agricultural products into income. The

---

[31]Samuel Heywood and Capel Lofft. *The Right of Protestant Dissenters to a Compleat Toleration Asserted Containing an Historical Account of the Test Laws, and Shewing the Injustice, Inexpediency, and Folly of the Sacramental Test . . . With an Answer to the Objection from the Act of Union with Scotland* (London: J. Johnson, 1789), 23.

[32]Blethen and Curtis, 16.

only product that farmers in Ireland could export to the British mainland was wool. They were forbidden from exporting all other goods, especially livestock. Beyond wool, the only product that managed to sustain growers was flax, which was an integral part of linen production.[33]

    The wool and linen business kept a steady flow of ships moving between Londonderry and Belfast and major ports in the North American colonies. During periods of low flax demand, ships' captains sought out ways to make money for the return trip to the colonies, and Scots-Irish farmers looking for new opportunities fit the bill. Some of these farmers paid their own way with what they had left; others sold themselves into indenture, usually a seven-year term of servitude to American planters. By the mid eighteenth-century, several colonies had established incentives designed to lure these Scots-Irish farmers to their lands. The colonies offered cheap land and typically paid ship captains for their human cargo, creating dangerous incentives for the captains to compromise safety in favor of profit. In one of the extreme cases, the owners of the 80-ton ship *Nancy* advertised her as a 300-ton brig. Ideally, the 80-ton ship could have supported less than 100 passengers, but in late 1767, she transported almost 300 passengers from Belfast to Charleston.[34] It is difficult to imagine what the conditions could have been like aboard the *Nancy*, but Henry Laurens, a future President of the Revolutionary Congress and a man well acquainted with the slave trade, found the conditions so shocking to his senses that he wrote:

---

    [33]Ibid., 18.

    [34]Wayne Hannah and Maureen Dorcy Hannah, *A Hannah Family of West Virginia* (Shelton, WA: W. and M. Hannah, 2000), 6-7.

> I never saw an instance of Cruelty in ten or twelve Years experience in that branch equal to the Cruelty exercised upon those poor Irish. . . . Self Interest prompted the Baptized heathen in the first case to take care of the wretched Slaves for a Market, but no other care was taken of those poor Protestant Christians from Ireland but to deliver as many as possible alive on Shoar [sic] upon the cheapest terms, no matter how they fared upon their Voyage nor in what condition they were landed.[35]

Despite the deplorable conditions, the six to ten-week voyage, and the two-week quarantine in the colonial port-of-call, the Scots-Irish came to America in droves. In some cases the flood of immigrants caught American colonial officials by surprise. William Penn's secretary for the colony of Pennsylvania, James Long, exclaimed, "It looks as if Ireland is to send all its inhabitants hither."[36] As the influx of poor Scots-Irish continued, an official in the same colony is said to have observed that the colony had "more Irish than people."[37] Of the approximately 250,000 immigrants who came to the Americas from the British Isles between 1717 and 1800 about 210,000 were Scots-Irish from Ulster.[38]

Those Scots-Irish settlers departing Ulster for the colonies in the early to mid eighteenth-century came predominantly to Pennsylvania. Evidence of their mass arrival can be seen in the large number of towns in the colony that bore Irish place names. As the Scots-Irish settled in the new world, they named their new homes after their old homes: Londonderry, Belfast, and Antrim. While this large movement to one colony was

---

[35]Arthur Mitchell, *South Carolina Irish* (Charleston, SC: History Press, 2011), 25.

[36]Kerby A. Miller, *Ireland and Irish America: Culture, Class, and Transatlantic Migration* (Dublin: Field Day in association with the Keough-Naughton Institute for Irish Studies at the University of Notre Dame, 2008), 127.

[37]McCarthy, 26.

[38]Blethen and Curtis, 20.

influenced to some degree by the sheer number of ships that called upon the ports along the Delaware River, it is likely that other qualities drove the Scots-Irish to gravitate towards Pennsylvania. The colony was well known for their religious toleration, and their predominant use of the indenture system also made it an attractive destination for migration. It did not take long for the prime land surrounding Philadelphia to be taken up, or to garner such high prices that the poor immigrants could not afford it. As the flood of Scots-Irish immigrants showed no signs of slowing, they began to move west, into Chester and then Lancaster counties. Adventurous, or sometimes destitute, settlers moved even further west, living among the Conestoga and the Shawnee Indians.

It was not long before these settlers began to abandon their lands and move on. Some were perhaps younger sons whose inheritance did not seem promising, and some were probably leaving land that had been worn out by irresponsible farming practices. Others had never been officially deeded the land that they were living on, and as small communities turned into townships and then villages, the squatters had to leave. While many Scots-Irish stayed in Pennsylvania for generations, countless others left and headed south. Those who left did not spread to the four winds, but rather followed a predictable migration pattern. The first major stopping point along the Great Wagon Road of the backcountry was Augusta County, Virginia.[39] Today, Augusta County is the area surrounding Staunton, but in the mid eighteenth-century, the county consisted of the entire Shenandoah Valley and lands well to the west. Up until the late 1720s, few people had ventured beyond the Blue Ridge Mountains to settle on the fertile land within the

---

[39]David Kennedy, Lizabeth Cohen, and Thomas Andrew Bailey, *The American Pageant: A History of the American People. Vol. I* (Boston. MA: Wadsworth Cengage Learning, 2010), 90.

valley. Other than a large German presence from Pennsylvania, few had wanted to risk living so far from civilization with various Indian tribes nearby. During this same time, Virginia sought to create a buffer in the valley, which would provide the large landholders in the Tidewater with a greater degree of security from Indian raids. Two men were granted massive tracts of land within the valley for the expressed purpose of enticing settlers to the land.[40] The Scots-Irish responded to the offers of inexpensive land and came in large numbers, settling heavily within the upper valley from Staunton to Big Lick (which today is known as Roanoke).

From the late 1720s through the late 1740s this land rapidly filled up with Scots-Irishmen who had until recently been farming in Pennsylvania. By the 1750s, the upper Shenandoah Valley was beginning to look a lot like the parts of Pennsylvania that the Scots-Irish had left. The vast untamed valley had become civilized with townships and villages, and the best lands already owned. Instead of returning to Pennsylvania, the Scots-Irish next headed farther south, from Roanoke towards the North Carolina Piedmont. The population of the Piedmont and Appalachians of North Carolina exploded from the 1750s to the outbreak of the War for Independence. In 1750, the incorporated parts of North Carolina extended west only as far as modern Caswell County down to modern Richmond County. By 1775, the incorporated parts of the colony extended as far west as modern Surry County in the north, down to current Cherokee County in the far

---

[40]Blethen and Curtis, 39.

southwest.[41] Overwhelmingly, the residents in these new counties were Scots-Irish settlers who had arrived within the previous several decades.[42]

In the late 1750s, the General Assembly of South Carolina was paying close attention to Virginia's attempts to populate its frontier backcountry with poor Scots-Irish settlers. South Carolina was seeking to provide a buffer between the Cherokee in the western foothills and the wealthy English and French Huguenot planters of the low country. Rather than selling backcountry land inexpensively to encourage settlement, the General Assembly went one step further and offered 100 acres of land free to every head of household, plus an additional 50 acres for every dependant. This drew large numbers of Scots-Irish down from Pennsylvania, Virginia and North Carolina, but the General Assembly also heavily advertised the offers in the north of Ireland. From 1730 to 1768, South Carolina intermittently made this offering and by the late 1760s even offered free equipment to help prospective farmers clear their newly acquired land.[43] The requirements to be eligible for the land were simple. The applicants needed to profess themselves poor Protestants, and then be able to clear 2 acres of land per year. Quitrents were even postponed for several years until the farmers could make their lands

---

[41] The Newberry Library, "North Carolina Historical Counties," http://historical-county.newberry.org/website/North_Carolina/viewer.htm (accessed October 24, 2013).

[42] Blethen and Curtis, 41.

[43] Janie Revill, *A Compilation of the Original Lists of Protestant Immigrants to South Carolina, 1763-1773* (Baltimore: Genealogical Pub. Co, 1974), 3-5.

productive. Even when quitrents were required, few immigrants paid them, and if they did, costs were minimal.[44]

The deal offered by South Carolina was so enticing that not only did large numbers of Scots-Irish continue flowing south from Pennsylvania, but also large numbers came from Ulster through Charleston.[45] The Scots-Irish were not the only group of poor Protestants to take up South Carolina's offer. Large numbers of ethnic Germans settled in the crook of land between the Broad and Saluda rivers, founding what became known as the Dutch Fork.[46] Poor English settlers found homes speckled throughout the backcountry and a small number of Welsh settlers moved in along the Enoree River. Despite this variety of ethnic groups that came to South Carolina during this time, the Scots-Irish were the undisputed majority. Names like Calhoun, McKinley, Caldwell and Murray were the norm in the backcountry.

A People Apart

By the eve of the American Revolution, the people who became known as the Scots-Irish overwhelmingly populated the colonial backcountry from the Savannah River all the way to the Susquehanna River. They were a people roughly 1,600 years in the making. From the Irish domination of the Picts to the Plantation of Ulster, they rarely

---

[44]Alvin Rabushka, *Taxation in Colonial America* (Princeton: Princeton University Press, 2009), 701.

[45]James Byrne, Philip Coleman, and Jason King, *Ireland and the Americas: Culture, Politics, and History: a Multidisciplinary Encyclopedia* (Santa Barbara, CA: ABC-CLIO, 2008), 847.

[46]Nancy Rose and George Mendenhall Wilson, *George and Son: A Legacy of Letters* (Indianapolis, IN: Dog Ear Pub, 2009), 81.

lived in well-governed lands. They had endured hundreds of years of warfare, and were constantly facing dangers from neighbors who detested them. This set of circumstances, combined with their dissenting Protestant creeds, contributed to their tribal behavior. Scots-Irish usually moved in family groups; moreover, it was common for all the sons of one family to marry all the daughters of another, further linking the family groups and strengthening their insular identity. The massive migrations of the early medieval, early modern and colonial eras, along with their fervent nonconformist religious views truly created the Scots-Irish as a people apart.

CHAPTER 3

BREAKING THE BACKCOUNTRY

The colonial backcountry that Scots-Irish immigrants settled in was never an entirely stable place to live. Tensions between the English settlers and the American Indians had been fluid since the first settlers ventured into the North American interior. In 1642, relations between Virginia settlers and the local Indians were particularly strained. Settlers looking to travel into the interior of Virginia were expected to either have sufficient means to defend themselves, or to hire armed parties to travel with them for their protection. People who had made no provision for their own defense were either fined or otherwise punished.[47] Despite these early tensions, relations were not always adversarial between the backcountry settlers and their Indian neighbors. It was the decades prior to the vigilante movements of the 1760s that saw significant degradation of backcountry stability.

Prior to the 1750s, the South Carolina backcountry presented an incredibly diverse mixture of European colonists and Cherokee and Creek Indians. Borders between "Indian Country" and the "Colonies" were blended and unclear. The economy of the backcountry was in many cases just as diverse and complex as the bustling international economy of Charleston. It depended heavily on interactions between the European colonists and their neighboring Indian tribes. This backcountry economy went well beyond simple fur trading. Intermarriage between Cherokees and Scots-Irish settlers was not uncommon, and Creeks along the Savannah River were often paid to hunt down

---

[47]Clayton Cramer, *Armed America: The Remarkable Story of How and Why Guns Became As American As Apple Pie* (Nashville, TN: Nelson Current, 2006), 4.

runaway slaves and return them to their masters. As gifted herders, Indians were often hired to shepherd livestock from the backcountry down to the Charleston markets.[48] Scots-Irish settlers in the well-populated lands between the low country and the frontier beyond the Broad and Saluda Rivers were producers of tobacco that was consumed by both the low country elite and the Cherokee beyond the mountains to their west.[49] Further north in the colony of Pennsylvania, Indian-Colonial relations were equally complex and layered. Many Indians in Pennsylvania were Christian converts and fairly westernized. The Conestoga were a group of Susquehannoch Indians who had converted to Christianity and were even particularly fond of giving their children the English names of prominent Pennsylvania settlers.

A number of conditions combined to sour an already tenuous relationship between the European settlers of the British colonies and their Indian neighbors. William Penn, the proprietor of the colony of Pennsylvania, was committed to respecting the traditional land rights of the Indians within the land granted to him by Charles II. He was attempting to institute a utopia in the new world, one managed according to his Quaker principles. These principles led him to deal with the numerous native tribes in as fair a manner as he could. In 1701, negotiations were made for the peaceful and equitable purchase of lands from the Susquehanna, the Shawnee, and the Onondaga.[50] For many

---

[48] Joshua Piker, "Colonists and Creeks: Rethinking the Pre-Revolutionary Southern Backcountry," *The Journal of Southern History* 70, no. 3 (August 2004): 503-540.

[49] John W. Gordon, *South Carolina and the American Revolution: A Battlefield History* (Columbia: University of South Carolina Press, 2003), 18.

[50] Kevin Kenny, *Peaceable Kingdom Lost: The Paxton Boys and the Destruction of William Penn's Holy Experiment* (Oxford: Oxford University Press, 2009), 11.

years, Pennsylvania was able to exist without a militia because of the warm relations between the European settlers and their Indian neighbors. The settlers dealt with the local Indians fairly, conducted regular and lucrative trade with them, and in turn the local tribes protected the settlers from perimeter tribes that might attempt to raid their settlements.[51]

It did not take long, however, for Penn's Holy Experiment to tarnish. William Penn died in 1718 and the ideals he hoped would guide the settlement of his colony appear to have died with him. His sons, Thomas, Richard and John, inherited the colony and immediately set about turning it into a business venture rather than continue their father's vision of a Holy Experiment. William's son, Thomas, seemed particularly detached from his father's Quaker beliefs. Shortly after his father's death, he left the Quaker faith and became an Anglican. The hopes that the Pennsylvania Indians held for living peaceably with their European neighbors waned in the 1730s. In what has been called the worst land fraud in American history, the Penn brothers manipulated, swindled and cheated the Delawares out of a massive amount of land in a transaction known as the Walking Purchase.[52]

In addition to the confusion and anger caused by the Walking Purchase, even legitimate land transactions between the Delaware tribe and colonial authorities were often sources of tension between the two. Generally, American Indians had a very different concept of land ownership than their European counterparts. There were many cases of Delaware groups offering to sell tracts of land that had been sold by their

---

[51]Fred Anderson, *The War That Made America: A Short History of the French and Indian War* (New York: Viking, 2005), 11-12;

[52]Matthew C. Ward, *Breaking the Backcountry: The Seven Years' War in Virginia and Pennsylvania, 1754-1765* (Pittsburgh, PA: University of Pittsburgh Press, 2003), 25.

ancestors a generation prior. It was in this way that much of the Walking Purchase was made. The Penn brothers managed to produce a paper documenting the sale of the land in question sometime near the end of the seventeenth-century. During this same time, the arrival of the first waves of Scots-Irish settlers into the Pennsylvania backcountry only complicated the situation. In many cases, these settlers fled from their indentures early, or could not afford the quitrents for the lands granted them after their indentures. Others simply decided that the lands they had been apportioned did not meet their needs. The result was countless Scots-Irishmen settling on lands that were generally agreed to belong to local Indians.

The outbreak of war between England and France in 1754 was far more significant in contributing to the deterioration of Euro-Indian relations in the colonial backcountry. The French and Indian War,[53] as it became known, was a culmination of tensions between the French and English colonial authorities as both sought to expand their land claims well into the Ohio valley and beyond. Caught in the middle were the American Indians, as they struggled to decide whether to choose sides or remain neutral. Throughout the late 1740s, as tensions between the French and English increased, the Iroquois Confederacy tried to remain neutral. Tanaghrishan, the essentially powerless but diplomatically perceptive "Half-King" of the Iroquois, attempted to play the two European powers against each other. He quickly found that he was attempting to play an

---

[53]The French and Indian War was the North American theater of the much larger Seven Years' War, which was fought between all the major powers of Europe and Russia. For a time even Sweden and the Mughal Empire were involved on the side of France.

age-old game in which both European sides had far more experience than he did and decided that the Iroquois interests were best served in assisting their British neighbors.[54]

The Iroquois believed that allying with the British would give them the economic advantage that they needed in order to secure their control over the Delaware. The Iroquois were the *de jure* masters of the Delaware because of conquests from generations past, but their control over these other tribes had lessened as a result of their own short-sightedness. As the Penn brothers sought to expand their land ownership within Pennsylvania, they had chosen to work solely with the Iroquois since they were typically easier to negotiate with, and had no ancestral ties to the lands occupied by their vassal tribes. The Iroquois had no reservations about selling the lands out from underneath the Delaware, seeing a great deal of benefit with very little cost to themselves. The problems came when the Delaware were forced to move beyond the range of effective control of the Iroquois. In 1748, at a treaty meeting in Logstown, Pennsylvania, representatives of the various Ohio tribes attempted to circumvent the Confederacy and deal with the Pennsylvania colonial representatives directly. The open willingness of the Delaware leaders to operate independent of their Iroquois masters frightened the Half-King. He decided that an alliance with the British would put the Iroquois in a place to gain the trade goods needed to maintain at least economic control over the Delaware and Shawnee.

The tribes of the Ohio valley, were well versed in English land acquisition techniques. Since the 1730s, Delaware and Mingo Indians had arrived in the Ohio valley, telling stories of the swindling ways of the English settlers. Although they would have

---

[54]Anderson, *The War that Made America*, 17-24.

likely preferred to stay out of the conflict between the two European superpowers, since the lands they occupied were the very lands at the heart of the conflict, they knew they had to choose sides. The French were traditional trading partners with the Ohio Indians and never showed much interest in colonizing any of the lands in which they operated, which made them appealing as allies. Although the European settlers further south in the Carolinas were mostly unmolested throughout the French and Indian War, the conflict was a continental one for the Native Americans. In the backcountry of Virginia and the Carolinas, the Catawba and Cherokee Indians were eager to take advantage of the opportunity to fight their rivals, the Shawnee. For generations the Ohio Indians had traveled down the path that ultimately became the Great Wagon Trail, raiding tribes all the way to the Savannah River.[55] The Cherokee, frequent targets of Shawnee raiding parties, were all too happy to come to the aid of the British in the ensuing war.[56] In many ways, the role that the Native Americans played in the French and Indian War constituted a separate but aligned conflict. Early on in the war, both the French and the English discovered that managing the native warriors presented an almost insurmountable challenge.

The challenge that the English had in coordinating efforts with their native allies was, to some degree, responsible for the commencement of open hostilities between the two European powers. In the summer of 1753, the Governor of Virginia, Robert

---

[55]The Great Wagon Trail ran from Philadelphia, west through Lancaster and then roughly southwest through Harper's Ferry to Winchester, Va. From Winchester the trail train down the Shenandoah valley to Roanoke before splitting west into Kentucky, and southeast to the Carolina Piedmont and on to Augusta, Georgia on the Savannah River.

[56]Michael N. McConnell, *A Country between: The Upper Ohio Valley and Its Peoples, 1724-1774* (Lincoln: University of Nebraska Press, 1997), 48-50.

Dinwiddie received word of French movements in the Ohio valley. The French had been busy that spring, constructing three forts in the valley, stretching from Fort Presque Isle along the southern shore of Lake Erie to Fort Machault at the confluence of the French Creek and Allegheny River. Dinwiddie was convinced that their ultimate goal was to gain a stronghold along the forks of the Ohio. The Governor was financially involved with the Ohio Company of Virginia that was seeking to establish a trading post on the forks, and thereby increase the influence of Virginia on the ill-defined frontiers of the Ohio Valley.[57] In response to this bold display by the French, Dinwiddie was given broad authority by the English Crown to evict the French from the disputed region by any means necessary. Unfortunately for him, however, he had been spending the last legislative session creating an enemy within the House of Burgesses over details of his compensation as Governor. The toxic relationship that had grown between the Governor and the House resulted in complete legislative gridlock. Dinwiddie's hopes of building a Virginian fort at the forks of the Ohio to stop the French incursion were dashed because of his own greed.[58] With the strongest means for securing English control over the Ohio valley locked in debate in the Virginia House of Burgesses, Governor Dinwiddie turned to a 21-year-old Virginia militia Major well known for his skills as a frontier surveyor.

Major George Washington, along with Tanaghrishan and a pair of Mingo chiefs left in the late fall of 1753. By December, he had successfully reconnoitered the French forts along the Allegheny and found them well-manned and fully prepared for the winter. More disturbingly, he found them prepared to continue their military expedition toward

---

[57]Ward, 26-28.

[58]Anderson, *The War that Made America*, 39.

the Forks of the Ohio. Unsurprisingly, when Washington met with the French officer in charge of Fort LeBoeuf, the Frenchman politely declined to vacate the forts. All Major Washington could do was return to Williamsburg and brief the Governor on the distressing state of affairs. Armed with information of impending French incursion on the Forks, Governor Dinwiddie was able to get the House of Burgesses to provide funds for the pay and provisioning of a regiment of provincial troops, and for the construction of a fort at the Forks of the Ohio.[59] The task of constructing the fort was contracted to the Ohio Company of Virginia. William Trent, John Fraser, and Edward Ward of the Ohio Company set out to the Forks of the Ohio in hopes of constructing a fort there before the French could continue their military expedition. The three entrepreneurs wasted no time; the foundations of a fort were already well underway by late February 1754. Back in Virginia, the task of raising a new provincial regiment fell on the shoulders of the newly promoted Lieutenant Colonel Washington.[60]

Washington and his men set out for the Forks in early April. They were undermanned, poorly equipped, and untrained. Shortly before Trent, Fraser, and Ward finished construction on the Fort that Washington was on his way to protect, the French arrived and the loss of the fort was merely a matter of words.[61] By the end of May,

---

[59]Ibid., 43.

[60]Eric Hinderacker and Peter C. Mancall, *At the Edge of Empire: The Backcountry in British North America* (Baltimore: Johns Hopkins University Press, 2003), 101-103.

[61]Although the workers of the Ohio Company were capable of defending themselves from raiding parties, they were in no shape to defend themselves against a military force. They handed over the fort and were allowed to head back to Virginia. The French, in turn finished the construction, turning the fort into one of the largest fortifications in North America at that time.

Washington was camped not far from the French fort when he received word of a French scouting party nearby. Tanaghrishan and his warriors scouted out their location before guiding Washington and a few of his Virginians forward to assess the situation. The Virginians set themselves in a position on high ground overlooking the French scouting camp. Before Washington could decide on what to do about the French party, a nervous soldier discharged his musket, triggering a full volley of musket fire on the unsuspecting French. Tanaghrishan and the Mingo warriors sat back until Washington was able to get control over his soldiers and order a cease-fire. The French soldiers were caught completely by surprise. A number of them were wounded by the volley, including their leader, Lieutenant Joseph Coulon de Villiers de Jumonville. Once the Virginians had regained their composure, Tanaghrishan and the Mingos descended on the stunned and wounded Frenchmen, killing and scalping almost all of them. Tanaghrishan himself found Jumonville lying on his back, severely wounded in the chest. The Iroquois Half-King stood over Jumonville and spoke to him in French, "*Tu n'es pas encore mort, mon pére.*"—"Thou art not yet dead, my father."[62] With that, Tanaghrishan split open Jumonville's skull with his tomahawk, killing him. The Half-King knew that if Washington was able to salvage a diplomatic resolution out of the accident, the Iroquois would likely lose the opportunity to expand their control over the Delaware Indians. Although the Iroquois were allies of the English, their ultimate goals were not precisely aligned, and Washington discovered just how complicated Indian partnerships could be.[63]

---

[62] Anderson, *The War that Made America*, 47.

[63] Fred Anderson, *Crucible of War: The Seven Years' War and the Fate of Empire in British North America, 1754-1766* (New York: Alfred A. Knopf, 2000), 56-57.

The English were not the only ones to discover how unmanageable Indian warriors could be as allies in the conflict. Three years after the murder of Jumonville by the Iroquois Half-King, the French commander Louis-Joseph de Montcalm would lose control of his Indian allies, resulting in the massacre of defenseless surrendering British forces. Montcalm was commander of a large column of French soldiers and Indian warriors based in Montreal. In August of 1756, his forces captured Fort Oswego on the southern coast of Lake Erie. A year later, Montcalm set his sights on Fort William Henry on the northern coast of Lake George, just south of Lake Champlain. The French forces were able to surround Fort William Henry, cutting the line of communication to the larger Fort Edward to the south. After a brief skirmish between Montcalm's forces and a reinforcing group of Massachusetts militia, Montcalm demanded that the British commander of Fort William Henry surrender.

The British commander, the Scots-Irish Lieutenant Colonel George Monro refused and dispatched a messenger to Fort Edward requesting additional reinforcements. The commander of Fort Edward did not want to risk further disaster by sending more forces toward a losing situation. A messenger tried to make it back to Fort William Henry, but he did not make it safely. Indian scouts found the messenger and killed him, allowing the French commander to intercept the message. Armed with the knowledge that Monro would not be receiving any reinforcements, he decided to lay siege to the fort, systematically digging trenches closer to the fort until their large mortars were in range of the fortification's walls. After a six-day siege, the walls of Fort William Henry began to fail against the pounding of the French artillery. Colonel Monro could see that the situation was hopeless and surrendered to Montcalm on August 7th, 1757. The terms of the surrender were typical of European armies at the time. Monro's force would be allowed to retain their colors and their muskets. One cannon could be taken along with Monro, but no ammunition was allowed. Monro would march towards Fort Edward and none of his soldiers were to resume fighting for a year. The Indian allies of Montcalm, predominantly Huron, were confused by these terms. They felt as if they had done most of the hard work required to trap the British force at the fort and were upset that they were not allowed to take captives, which was the custom in Indian warfare. Their response to these terms was to ignore them. While a few of the tribes that accompanied Montcalm's forces simply left, returning for their villages, most stormed the fort, attacking the sick and wounded British that remained. The retreating British force did not fare much better than the wounded left at Fort William Henry. While the British Regulars managed to escape the worst of the Hurons' wrath, the Provincial soldiers, all Americans, were attacked multiple times as they attempted to retreat back to Fort Edward. Ultimately Indians killed about 200 soldiers and camp followers, and carried off as prisoners an estimated 300.[64] Montcalm's inability to control his Indian allies had strategic consequences. The British, convinced that Montcalm had encouraged his Indian warriors to perpetrate the massacre, refused to honor requests for prisoner transfers, and Monro's regiment was sent directly back to service rather than remaining out of action for the requisite year.

The provincial American troops were horrified by the slaughter on their march from Fort William Henry to Fort Edward; their families at home were also feeling the wrath of Indians executing a total war strategy. Although American Indians fought in

---

[64] Anderson, *Crucible of War*, 167-169.

almost every major battle during the French and Indian War, these major battles were not the full extent of their involvement. In the frontier settlements of Pennsylvania, the European settlers found themselves the object of much more frequent Indian raids. Although many would assume that the Indian raids would focus on Scots-Irish settlements well within Indian lands, the overwhelming majority of the raids within Pennsylvania were directed at ethnic Germans who were settled along the frontier.[65] One common quality of the targeted settlements was their adherence to faiths that espoused nonviolence and prohibited military service. In a roughly two and a half year period from 1755-1757, over 350 civilians were murdered in only a few areas of northwest Berks county, and northern Lancaster county. A roughly equal number of civilians were taken captive.[66] These murders are counted completely separately from deaths that occurred when area militias encountered Indian raids. Two incidences from 1757 in the village of Bethel illustrate the nature of these attacks.

On May 16th, 1757, Johannes Spitler, a Mennonite immigrant from Switzerland was mending a broken fence on his property just south of Bethel, along the Little Swatara Creek. A group of Indians attacked him, shooting and scalping him. His wife, Elizabeth, fired a rifle from the front porch of their house, temporarily scattering the raiding Indians. She escaped with her children to her father's farm roughly a mile away, only to watch her own home burn in the distance. Her husband's body was later found on their property,

---

[65]"Lists of Pennsylvania Settlers Murdered, Scalped and Taken Prisoners by Indians, 1755-1756," *The Pennsylvania Magazine of History and Biography* 32, no. 3 (1908): 309-319.

[66]Ibid.

horribly mangled.[67] A year earlier, not far from Spitler's farm, Felix Wuench was plowing his farm when he met a similar fate.

> they crept up, unobserved, behind the fence of Felix Wuench, shot him through the breast, as he was ploughing; he cried lamentably and ran, but the Indians soon caught up to him, and, although he defended himself some time with his whip, they cut his head and breast with their tomahawks and scalped him. His wife, hearing his cries and the report of two guns, ran out of the house, but was soon taken away by the enemy who carried her away with them, together with one of her own and two of her sister's children, after setting the house on fire, and otherwise destroying property.[68]

Why the Indian raiders would have chosen to target groups of relatively inoffensive settlers like the Mennonites and Moravians is uncertain. While they were undoubtedly influenced to some degree by the fact that they knew the pacifists would not be well-equipped to defend themselves, it is likely that these groups were targeted for other reasons. The Moravians in particular were known for their evangelical missionary work with the Indians, successfully converting hundreds to Christianity. These converted Indians often took up European habits of dress, and even took European names. It is feasible that this cultural invasion was viewed by the Indians as even more dangerous than the ever expanding settlement. It is equally likely that the raids were a psychological operation, targeting the westernized Indians to prevent them from joining the English in the war against the French.

These raids of intimidation were not only conducted in the Pennsylvania backcountry. The Scots-Irish and German settlers in the northern Virginia backcountry were relentlessly terrorized during the war. The Shawnee and Delaware raiders were

---

[67]Daniel Rupp, *History of the Counties of Berks and Lebanon: Containing a Brief Account of the Indians* (Salem, MA: Higginson Book Co, 1992), 310-311.

[68]Ibid., 317.

attempting to prevent the Virginians from being able to successfully link up with the Catawba and Cherokee Indians to their southwest.[69] The Cherokee in particular were more than willing to come to the aid of the Virginian settlers. The Shawnee were long time foes of the Cherokee, and the predominantly South Carolina based tribe had long sought to get out from under the economic thumb of Charleston and engage in trade with the Virginians. The constant raiding by the Shawnee on the Virginian settlers had the desired effect however. The backcountry settlers were unable to discern one tribe from another and frequently attacked Cherokee war parties that were actually coming to assist them.[70] The cold reception that they received from the Virginians, and the lack of any gifts for the services they rendered naturally frustrated the Cherokee.

After partaking in multiple raids on Shawnee and French strongholds as far as Fort Duquesne and not being compensated by the British, the Cherokee decided to abandon their alliance with the English. As the Cherokee warriors made their way back to their lands, they took their compensation from helpless farmers in the Virginia and Carolina backcountry. In the wake of the failed alliance between the Cherokee and the British, the Cherokee nation became particularly fractured. Several factions emerged with divergent goals. Cherokee elder Attakullakulla stood at the head of an Anglophile group of Cherokee who still felt that they could work a beneficial relationship with the English settlers along the mid-Atlantic. South Carolina Governor William Lyttleton saw an opportunity in the fractured Cherokee nation, and in October of 1759, Lyttleton commissioned a punitive expedition charged with punishing the Cherokee for their abuse

---

[69] Ward, 50.

[70] Ibid., 60.

of backcountry families on their return from the Ohio valley. The expedition accomplished little beyond obtaining Cherokee prisoners. After many of the soldiers contracted smallpox, Lyttleton ordered the expedition's commander to make contact with Attakullakulla in order to secure a peace treaty under conditions beneficial to the government of South Carolina. The commander of the expedition was able to work out a peace treaty that ceded a large portion of Cherokee lands east of the mountains. Once the expedition returned, Lyttleton had the Cherokee prisoners executed.[71]

The farcical treaty made with Attakullakulla and the execution of Cherokee prisoners sent the backcountry region of the Carolinas and Virginia into chaos as the various other Cherokee factions banded together in response to the provocation. Although the Cherokee conducted raids from as far north as Augusta County, Virginia, to as far south as the Savannah River, there was no misunderstanding as to which their primary enemy was. The recently arrived Scots-Irish settlers of the Carolinas felt the brunt of their wrath.

The consequences of the French and Indian War were far reaching for the inhabitants of the colonial backcountry. In their unskilled attempts to use their Indian partners against their enemies, the French and English both failed to comprehend the role that inter-tribal diplomatic relations played in maintaining the fragile balance that had existed for decades between the Indians and their European neighbors. The result was a level of violence previously unknown in the backcountry. From the unconventional warfare of the Delaware and Shawnee in Pennsylvania, to the Cherokee War in the southern Colonies, the once lawless but promising lands that lay beyond the major cities

---

[71]Ibid., 196-197.

of the coast became a treacherous no-man's land that only the most self-reliant of families chose to remain in. It was in this chaotic environment that the Scots-Irish vigilante movements of the 1760s and 1770s emerged.

CHAPTER 4

THE PAXTON BOYS

At Wit's End

Paxtang, Pennsylvania, alternately called Paxton, is a suburb of Harrisburg in Dauphin County. It is part of a major metropolitan area along Interstate 76 between Philadelphia and Pittsburgh. Paxtang is situated along the Spring Creek and Slotznick Run on the eastern side of the Susquehanna River, just north of where the Swatara Creek connects. In 1763, in the aftermath of the French and Indian War, the village was hardly a bustling city, but stood alone in the far western frontier of European-settled Pennsylvania. Although Indian attacks on civilians in the Pennsylvania backcountry were focused on the pacifist Germans to the east, the Scots-Irish settlers of Paxton did not escape unscathed. Three months after raiders killed Johannes Spitler and Felix Wuench, Indians killed four Scots-Irishmen, and three others were carried off as captives. Two years prior to these episodes a particularly vicious attack, in which eight were killed, startled the inhabitants of Paxton.[72] As the war finally ended in February of 1763, little seemed to change in the eyes of the Scots-Irish of the Pennsylvania backcountry.

---

[72]Rupp, 309.

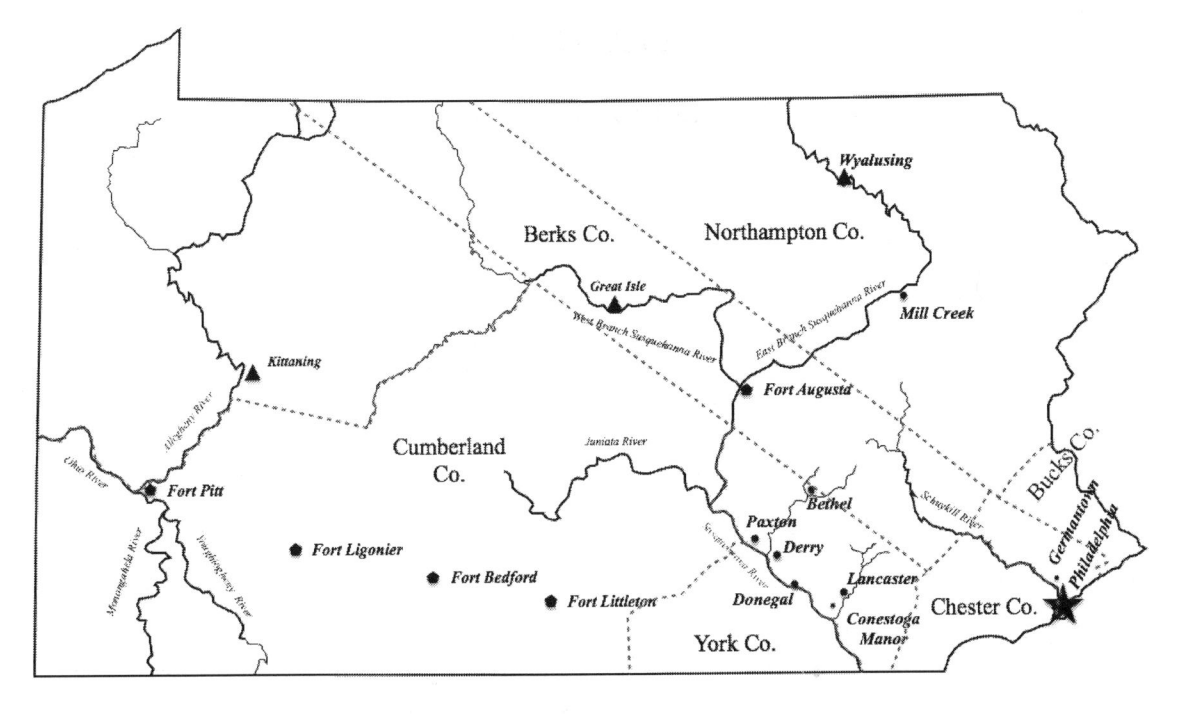

Figure 1. Map of Pennsylvania 1763, with selected settlements depicted.
Source: Created by author.

Without much delay after the conclusion of the Treaty of Paris,[73] another conflict erupted in many of the same locations that had seen the brunt of fighting during the French and Indian War. Although the French lost enormous land claims because of the war, their Indian allies were equal partners in loss. The British had negotiated a separate peace with the Shawnee and Delaware in late 1758, but by the time Montréal fell in the summer of 1760, the British began to treat the Ohio Valley Indians as conquered foes. Part of the agreement with the Ohio Valley Indians that had helped solidify the Treaty of

---

[73]The Treaty of Paris referenced here refers to the February 10th, 1763 treaty that concluded the colonial theater of the Seven Years War. This Treaty of Paris is not to be confused with one of the 22 other treaties from 1229 to 1951 bearing the same name. Among American readers, the Treaty of Paris is most often associated with the conclusion of the American Revolution in 1783.

Easton in 1758 was a British promise to curtail settlement beyond the Alleghenies. Whether or not the British actually intended to honor the agreement, settlers continued to pour into the Indian territories. The British also retained all the French forts that the Indians had assumed would be abandoned after the conflict. Most frustrating to the Indians however, was the refusal of British Major General Jeffery Amherst to continue the long tradition of gift-giving between the British and the Indians. The Indian economy had become heavily influenced by frequent gifts from the two major European powers, either vying for their loyalty, or at least encouraging their neutrality. The abrupt end of gift giving also had significant political implications for tribal chiefs. The understanding of most tribes was that the gifts were payment for being able to use their lands, and many Indians saw chiefs who could not extract gifts from the British as weak.[74] With the conclusion of the French and Indian war, Amherst felt that this was no longer necessary, and was a pointless expenditure.[75] This left the Indian economy in a lurch and created panic among many of the Indian communities closest to British settlements. The refusal of the British to trade gunpowder with the Indians was perhaps the most damaging. While the British engaged in gunpowder trade to help the Indians in their fight with the French, the Indians considered the gunpowder critical to their hunting. With the access to large quantities of cheap gunpowder cut off, further panic was created among the tribes.

At the same time that the British were antagonizing their native neighbors through abusive trade policies and continued encroachment on Indian lands, a cultural revival was

---

[74]Richard Middleton, *Pontiac's War: Its Causes, Course, and Consequences* (New York: Routledge, 2007), 21.

[75]Kenny, 115-117.

occurring in many tribes throughout the Ohio valley and all along the St. Lawrence River. The origins of this revival were the teachings of Neolin, a Delaware prophet. Neolin was convinced that the "Master of Life" was punishing the Indians because they had left their native culture and way of life behind, becoming dependant on the Europeans. He began preaching to his followers that the only way to improve their position was to cleanse themselves of European cultural habits and to evict the British from their ancestral lands. The emotional response to his teachings and the rapidity with which his message spread to other tribes resembled the Christian Great Awakening movement. Pontiac, another Delaware chief, agreed with Neolin, particularly in his belief that the British needed to be pushed off Indian lands. These two figures combined to lead to the largest organized Indian uprising in the eighteenth-century. Pontiac's Rebellion, as the movement came to be called, was a widespread Indian uprising involving a number of tribes in the Northeast. Attacks were launched on British forts from Fort Ouiatenon, northwest of modern Indianapolis, all the way to Fort Bedford in Pennsylvania. In all, thirteen British forts were attacked, and the Indians successfully took eight. Just as was the case in the French and Indian war, however, the Indian warriors did not limit their activity to British military strongholds. The Delaware in particular continued their attacks against settlers along the Susquehanna River. Some of their raids cut as deep into Pennsylvania as the outskirts of Philadelphia. The areas around Paxton, just becoming accustomed to peace, once again prepared for war.

  Pennsylvania found itself in a poor state to react to the renewed Indian violence. Partly due to a constrained fiscal environment, and partly due to the Quaker influence within the Assembly, Pennsylvania disbanded the militia and ceased offering bounties for

Indian scalps for some time.[76] Only a small detachment of British regulars remained in the colony, but they were to remain in Philadelphia for defense of the capital city. Without a paid militia or scalp bounties, it was difficult for the backcountry inhabitants to fend off the Indian threat. For a man to leave his farming responsibilities long enough to campaign against their native enemies meant potentially losing a season's worth of crops and his family's livelihood. Militias were expensive and needed to remain active for long periods of time in order to be effective. From the perspective of the backcountry settlers, the preferred method would have been reinstating the scalp bounties.[77] Without scalp bounties or a militia, backcountry settlers were reluctant to venture far from their farms, which were their livelihoods. This left the settlers in a state in which every family had to defend their own property. In the mid-summer of 1763, the Pennsylvania Colonial Assembly voted to raise a small 700-man militia regiment, of which, only 300 were dedicated to backcountry defense. The remainder was to focus on defending the core settlements within the colony.[78] Administrators divided the 300-man militia unit into two battalions; one in Lancaster County, and another in Cumberland County. Command of the Lancaster battalion fell on the shoulders of Rev. John Elder of the Paxton Presbyterian Church. Rev. Elder was of Scottish birth but had been living among the predominantly Scots-Irish community of Paxton and Donegal since the early 1740s. A

---

[76]Ibid., 119 and 164.

[77]Matthew Smith, *A Declaration and Remonstrance of the Distressed and Bleeding Frontier Inhabitants of the Province of Pennsylvania* (Philadelphia: W. Bradford, 1764), 16.

[78]Ibid., 119.

staunch Calvinist, Elder was of the Knoxian school of Presbyterian thought.[79] In the violent years of the French and Indian War, and Pontiac's Rebellion, he was known to preach with his rifle leaning against the pulpit, earning him the nickname "The Fighting Parson."[80] The authorities appointed Elder as Lieutenant Colonel of the battalion for his charisma and popularity in the backcountry, not necessarily for his tactical prowess. At 57 years old, Elder was expected to recruit rather than to lead his battalion of men in the field.

He split his battalion into two ranging companies of 50 men each. The two companies further subdivided into several small groups of men who created a rather porous defensive perimeter all around the Susquehanna Valley near Paxton. With so few men, all Elder could hope to do was discourage Indian attacks by having his men focus on the mountain passes into the valley. If one small group of his rangers were attacked, however, it was difficult for enough of the groups to converge in order to provide mutual defense. With such thin protection, the attacks continued. Elder and his rangers quickly concluded that a defensive posture with so few men was ineffective; to have any real impact on the Indian raiding parties, they would have to take a more offensive strategy.[81] In late August of 1763, without the authorization of colonial authorities, the Rev. Elder

---

[79]Helen Bruce Wallace, *Historic Paxton, Her Days and Her Ways, 1722-1913* (Harrisburg, PA: House of the Evangelical church, 1913), 68-77; Rod Gragg, *Forged in Faith* (New York: Howard Books, 2010), 171. Elder was exceedingly conservative in his theology, but like Knox saw the government as a means of oppression. He disliked the "New Side" Presbyterians for their similarities with the Baptists, but apparently willingly let his congregation peacefully split between "New Side" and "Old Side."

[80]Harrisburg Patriot News, "Fighting Parson Carried the Good Book and a Rifle," Sunday, 22 February 1976.

[81]Kenny, 125.

sent his rangers, now numbering perhaps twice their authorization, well beyond the confines of their normal defensive belt. The intended target of the rangers lay well up the west branch of the Susquehanna toward the Great Island Delawares northwest of Paxton. About 40 miles east of Great Island, they came upon what appeared to be an abandoned Indian village, although there was evidence of recent activity. Disappointed, the rangers believed they must have been detected shortly before their arrival. As they were preparing to depart, however, a group of Great Island Delaware ambushed them. The rangers managed to fend off the attack, but suffered four killed and six wounded themselves.[82]

Frustrated by their losses in the ambush, the Paxton Boys, as the group of rangers became known, became convinced that "friendly" Indians closer to Paxton must have warned the Great Island Delaware of their plans. As was all too often the case in frontier warfare, the Paxton Boys escalated their operations against all the local Indians. When they came upon vacant Indian settlements, they tore down the homes and burned the crops. In mid October, the Paxton Boys ranged further than ever before, initially intending to attack the Moravian Indians at Wyalusing. Before attacking at Wyalusing, Rev. Elder ordered his men to burn the corn crops of the New England settlers at Wyoming, since he feared they might be of use to the Delaware. On 17 October, just upriver from the Wyoming settlement, the Paxton boys came upon a Connecticut settlement named Mill Creek that had been attacked by a Delaware raiding party. The attack was so savage that it left images that did not soon leave the minds of the rangers who saw it. A pregnant woman roasted on a makeshift spit over a fire, hanging from

---

[82]Ibid., 126.

hooks driven through her hands. Several men had awls stabbed into their eye sockets. Everyone in the village had either fled or been killed, the homes burned, and the livestock scattered.[83] The attack on Mill Creek seemed to have had a serious impact on the morale of the Paxton Boys. After they discovered the destroyed village, they began taking out their frustrations on any Indians they happened to encounter when they were out ranging. For example, a small group of Moravian Indians were returning from a trading trip in eastern settlements when the Paxton Boys attacked them, killing them all and feeling quite proud of their triumph over a small band of westernized Christian Indians.[84]

The Massacre of the Conestoga

The savagery of both the Paxton Boys and the Delawares continued for the remainder of the year, but two attacks on groups of Conestoga Indians by the Paxton Boys stood out as more savage than any others. Rev. Elder continued to enflame the fires of anger felt by the Scots-Irish Presbyterians, selecting passages from the Bible to provide religious affirmation for their behavior. During this same time, however, Rev. Elder seems to have lost some control over the unit that he helped create. Although Elder tailored his sermons to provoke anger against the Indians, he later claimed to have chided the rangers who had attacked Christian Indians. Abdicating his own personal responsibility for the militia unit, he wrote that the rangers ignored his exhortations and that he could do nothing to stop the more violent and unsanctioned attacks.[85] The Paxton

---

[83] John Brubaker, *Massacre of the Conestogas: On the Trail of the Paxton Boys in Lancaster County* (Charleston, SC: History Press, 2010), 33.

[84] Kenny, 133-134.

[85] Brubaker, 64.

Boys began assembling and ranging without any orders from Elder or their company commanders.

Late in the evening on 13 December 1763, the rangers again assembled without being called by their formal leadership. As heavy snow fell, somewhere between 50 and 60 men gathered in the town square before heading south out of Paxton and travelling along the Susquehanna river, intent on punishing the Indians settled at Conestoga Manor, just west of the town of Lancaster.[86] The weather that evening was particularly cold, and the snow continued to fall heavily, slowing their progress towards Conestoga Manor. The rangers decided to bed down near Harris' Mill, forcing themselves into the homes of many of the settlers nearby, invited, or not. Early in the morning, before sunrise, on the 14th, the rangers continued their march east towards the Indian village. They surrounded the village not long before sunrise, and found it completely quiet. All of the Conestoga were still asleep in their homes. Without any signal of warning, the Paxton rangers raced through the deep snow and descended on the sleeping Conestoga, murdering all six of the village's residents. The rest of the Conestoga were further east on trading trips with other settlements. The absence of the majority of the Conestoga accounts for the descriptions of the casualties of the massacre, elderly men, women, and at least one child.[87] As the rangers returned to Paxton, many of them stopped again to rest in the farmhouses of settlers along their path. One group of rangers stopped at the home of a Quaker family, not far from Conestoga Manor. The young son of the Quaker family noticed a toy gun

---

[86]Ibid., 17-18.

[87]Benjamin Franklin, *A Narrative of the Late Massacres, in Lancaster County, of a Number of Indians, Friends of this Province, By Persons Unknown* (Philadelphia: Anthony Ambruster, 1764), 1-4.

tied to the saddle of one of the rangers. He recognized the toy as belonging to one of the young Conestoga children with whom he frequently played. Once the rangers had rested and eaten, they left, the father of the family traveled to Conestoga Manor, discovering the massacre.[88]

Word of the massacre traveled quickly, and Pennsylvania officials quickly rounded up the remaining Conestoga villagers and placed them in protective custody in Lancaster, fearing that if they returned to Conestoga Manor, they too would be killed. On 27 December, another much larger group of rangers assembled in Paxton and marched on Lancaster. The group, estimated to be as large as 200 men, rode into Lancaster on a Sunday morning as most of the town was in church services. They must have received word of where the Conestoga were being held because they rode straight to the jail. The Conestoga within the jail had no ability to get out and flee, so it took little effort for the rangers to break in and kill the remaining 14 Indians.[89]

The Paxton Boys March on Philadelphia

The Paxton Boys were puzzled and frustrated by Pennsylvania's unsympathetic response to their vicious attack on Conestoga Manor. Although their attack on the remaining Conestoga at Lancaster was meant to finish off the remains of a tribe that they felt had betrayed their trust, it is likely that the Lancaster attack was also meant as a threat to Philadelphia. The intended message was that if the government would not raise a force capable of defending their homes, they would defend their homes in whatever manner

---

[88]Brubaker, 23.

[89]Ibid., 37-39.

they saw fit. Based on the response of Benjamin Franklin, a prominent member of the Pennsylvania Assembly, the message was received. In mid January 1764, Franklin penned a pamphlet in response to the massacre of the Conestoga both at Conestoga Manor and at Lancaster. In his "A Narrative of the Late Massacres in Lancaster County," he painted a gruesome description of how he imagined the attacks took place. He purposefully used the Indians' Christian names to draw sympathy, and called for the Paxton Boys to be arrested and tried for murder. The motivations ascribed by Franklin to the Paxton Boys were bloodlust and a racist fear of anyone with "reddish brown skin and black hair"[90] Franklin's response was a clear attempt to get ahead of the ensuing "Pamphlet War" cycle and drive public sentiment against the backcountry vigilantes.

Franklin had good reason to try to turn the public opinion against the Paxton Boys, because on January 2nd a letter forwarded by Edward Shippen, the Penn family's representative for Lancaster County, warned of a dire threat to Philadelphia. The letter warned of a company of about 200 backcountry men preparing to march on Philadelphia, ostensibly with the intent to kill the Moravian Indians then held at Province Island. The populace within Philadelphia was unaccustomed to defending themselves or serving in colonial militias, and Franklin was likely painting the Paxton Boys as monsters to encourage the few non-pacifists within the city to organize and take up arms against the backcountry men then moving on the capital.

Whatever Franklin's motivations for writing his anti-Paxton pamphlet, the Assembly took quick action based on the letter from Shippen. The Moravian Indians were rounded up on Province Island and escorted by British Regulars from Thomas Gage

---

[90]Franklin, 3.

to the neighboring colony of New York. Somewhat puzzlingly, the Pennsylvania Assembly appeared to have neglected to coordinate with the New York Assembly, and the Governor refused to allow "so great a body of Indians, in number about one hundred & forty, to pass into this Province." The New York Assembly seemed to sympathize with the Paxton Boys, since they reasoned that settling these Indians within their colony would only add "greatly to the strength of a people, from who, His Majesty's Subjects have already suffered so much."[91] During the month of January, while the Moravian Indians were being shuttled to and then from New York, the threat of a backcountry uprising never materialized. By 24 January, the Moravian Indians returned to Philadelphia and were housed in the city barracks for their own protection.[92]

The first letter threatening a march on Philadelphia may have been serious, since after the resettling of the Moravian Indians, traders moving to and from the backcountry reported to their Philadelphia friends that the backcountry settlers were displeased and once they had "completed their Whole Companys they are determined to come down."[93]

On 4 February 1764, word came to Philadelphia that the long threatened march of the backcountry men was underway and would likely arrive the next day. Although Penn had received a small contingent of British regulars to protect the barracks, the initial rumors of the backcountry uprising indicated that their numbers were vastly larger than what the regulars could defend against. Setting aside their political differences, Benjamin

---

[91]Pennsylvania, *Colonial Records* (Philadelphia: J, Severns and Co, 1851), 121-122.

[92]Kenny, 148.

[93]Ibid., 149.

Franklin and John Penn conferred on how best to respond to the impending attack, and they uncharacteristically reached an agreement. Franklin was to raise a militia force and defend the city. Franklin agreed to raise the militia, but felt it would be more politically palatable for him to serve in the militia rather than lead it.[94]

Tensions within the city were high. In the early morning hours of 5 February, nervous night watchmen, who assumed that fires in the distance were the approaching backcountry men, sounded a false alarm. However, the night watchmen were not wrong by much, as the Paxton Boys arrived in Germantown, just 10 miles north of the city center, later that afternoon. Once rumors of the backcountry men's arrival in Germantown spread through the city, it was not long before trains of Quakers were seen leaving the city. Many Quakers undoubtedly left because their pacifist ideals forbade their involvement in potential violence, but many others left because they knew that they were the objects of the Paxton Boys' anger. Quakers had always been considered friends of the various Indians within the colony, but most vexing to the backcountry Scots-Irish was their harboring Indians believed to be involved in aiding the Delaware during Pontiac's Rebellion.[95] Still other Quakers, much to the surprise of their neighbors, took up arms and prepared to defend the city. In his journal, the well known and well respected Lutheran minister Henry Muhlenberg commented that, "it seemed strange that such preparations should be made against one's fellow citizens and Christians, whereas

---

[94] Walter Isaacson, *Benjamin Franklin: An American Life* (New York: Simon and Schuster, 2003), 213.

[95] Kenny, 154.

no one ever took so much trouble to protect from the Indians His Majesty's subjects and citizens on the frontier."[96]

The Paxton Boys remained at Germantown throughout the remainder of the 5th and 6th of February. Many accounts indicate that the Paxton Boys took out some of their frustrations on the inhabitants of the village, pretending to scalp men and breaking windows of homes. John Penn sent several religious emissaries to try to bring the backcountry men to their senses.[97] Whether these emissaries were successful, or whether the Paxton Boys were simply waiting for the remainder of their forces to gather at Germantown before continuing, remains unclear; however, Philadelphia was safe for the remainder of the 6th. Early in the morning on the 7th, John Penn sent out another delegation to meet with the Paxton Boys and attempt to reason with them and save Philadelphia from their mischief. This time, the delegation had more political and diplomatic experience. Led by Benjamin Franklin, the delegation also contained such key officials as the speaker of the Assembly, the Attorney General, and the Mayor of Philadelphia. Little is known of the content of the discussions between Franklin's delegation and the leaders of the Paxton Boys; however, the talks were successful, ending with the Paxton Boys agreeing to disperse. The agreement to disperse was not a wholesale surrender of the Paxton Boy's goals, but rather an agreement to enter further

---

[96]John Henry Paul Reumann, *Muhlenberg's Ministerium, Ben Franklin's Deism, and the Churches of the Twenty-First Century: Reflections on the 250th Anniversary of the Oldest Lutheran Church Body in North America* (Grand Rapids, MI: W. B. Eerdmans Pub. Co., 2011), 190.

[97]Kenny, 161-162.

negotiations. Two of the leaders of the backcountry men remained to draw up a list of grievances they hoped would be addressed by the assembly.

Motivations of the March

The two Paxton leaders, Matthew Smith and James Gibson, together submitted two documents to the assembly. The *Declaration* and the *Remonstrance* provide the only explanation for the Paxton Boys' march on Philadelphia actually written by admitted members of the Paxton Boys. The identities of the remainder of the Paxton Boys remain a mystery. Since the attack on the Conestogas was considered by many to be a serious crime, there was little reason for any of the attackers to come forward and place their names in the annals of history. In the wake of the meeting at Germantown, a flurry of pamphlets was published by people both supportive of and hostile to the Paxton Boys' actions against the Conestogas. From these pamphlets, we can infer a wide range of motivations for the vigilante attacks and subsequent march on Philadelphia, yet the documents written by Smith and Gibson provide the only motivations that can reliably be called representative of the whole.

The *Declaration* opens with a testimony of the loyalty of the frontier settlers to the British Crown, in opposition to the crown's enemies "openly avowed or more dangerously concealed under a Mask of falsly pretended Friendship."[98] The reference to false friendship was primarily aimed at the Conestoga, but was likely a thinly veiled attack on the loyalties of the Quakers, whose official name was the Society of Friends. These same people were calling for the arrest of the Paxton Rangers both because of the

---

[98]Smith, 4.

attack on the Conestogas and because of their defiance of the established colonial government in Philadelphia. The authors go on to explain the nefarious activities of the Indians whom they killed. Although no evidence exists corroborating their account, the Paxton Boys claimed the Conestoga were allied with the Delaware and provided the openly hostile Indians with key intelligence on settlements. They additionally claimed that some of the Conestoga were known to boast of having killed a number of frontier settlers. Particularly annoying to the authors was the fact that the Quakers of Philadelphia refused to provide General Amherst "one single Farthing against a Savage Foe" while they seemed all too happy to shower out "publick Money lavishly" to hire guards in order to "protect his Majesty's worst of Enemies, those falsly pretended Indian Friends."[99] Another vexing dichotomy was that despite ending the long held practice of paying bounties for the scalps of enemy Indians, the Assembly offered rewards in numerous occasions for the apprehension of frontiersmen who attacked and wounded friendly Indians. The *Declaration* generally paints a picture of a colonial government more concerned with the welfare of Indians than they were with frontier English subjects who paid taxes and served in frontier militias, providing for the security of the entire colony.

The *Declaration* is generally an introduction for the more organized *Remonstrance,* which was a listing of demands that the Paxton Boys hoped would be redressed. The *Remonstrance* contained nine grievances; generally listed in order of magnitude. Strangely, the first grievance listed by Smith and Gibson had nothing to do with the Conestoga or Indians at all. The chief complaint of the Paxton Boys as conveyed by their leaders was the inequity of representation within the Pennsylvania Assembly.

---

[99]Ibid., 6.

This could be seen as a means of essentially shifting the subject away from their brutal attacks on the Indians, yet the *Declaration* dealt directly with this issue, and a number of the later grievances in the *Remonstrance* address the concern over Indian violence. Furthermore, the facts of the issue of representation bear out the truth of the Paxton Boys' grievance. The four counties that comprised the Pennsylvania backcountry: Lancaster, York, Cumberland and Berks collectively only elected 10 representatives, while the eastern counties of Philadelphia, Chester and Bucks elected 26.[100] It might be assumed that this disparity of representation was due to differences in taxable population since representation was based on taxable households rather than total population. This assumption proves false, however, when the tax rolls of 1760 are reviewed. While the eastern counties had a majority of the taxable population (16,221), the frontier counties amounted to 15,443. If the frontier counties had been allotted representatives by the same ratio of representatives to taxable households as the eastern counties, they would have elected 23 rather than the paltry 10 they were allowed.[101] Although it is doubtful that the frontier inhabitants had access to the tax rolls, the situation seemed obviously "Oppressive, unequal and unjust, the Cause of many of our Grievances, and an infringement of our natural Privileges of Freedom and Equality."[102] In claiming the inequity of representation was the cause of many of their grievances, the frontiersmen undoubtedly understood that as long as they had no real representation within the

---

[100] Ibid., 11.

[101] Frank J. Cavaioli, "A Profile of the Paxton Boys: Murderers of the Conestoga Indians," *Journal of the Lancaster County Historical Society* 82, no. 3 (March 1983): 78.

[102] Smith, 11.

Assembly, they would never have any hope of resolving any of the issues that plagued the backcountry.

The second grievance addressed by Smith and Gibson had little to do with the Indians themselves, but rather with what the Pennsylvania Assembly desired to do with the perpetrators of the crime. In the wake of the first attack by the Paxton Boys at Conestoga Manor, it became clear to the Assembly that there was strong support within the backcountry counties for the rangers. Even the Germans Lutherans within the backcountry seemed to be tacitly supportive of the attacks.[103] Although many of the Germans in the backcountry were pacifists like the Quakers, the rough treatment that they experienced during the French and Indian War, and subsequent violence of Pontiac's Rebellion, lead them to overlook such atrocities as the Conestoga massacre if they made them safer.[104] With such wide backcountry support for what was, in the eyes of the Philadelphians, a barbaric and illegal action, the Assembly drafted a bill that would move to Philadelphia all trials for people accused of murdering Indians. The Paxton Boys correctly assumed that the Assembly drafted the bill with the expressed goal of convicting and punishing the Scots-Irish rangers. The language within the second grievance is in many ways more emotionally charged than the first:

> This is manifestly to deprive British Subjects of their known Privileges, to cast an eternal Reproach upon whole Counties, as if they were unfit to serve their Country in the Quality of Jury-Men, and to contradict the well known Laws of the British Nation, in a point whereon Life, Liberty, and Security essentially depend:

---

[103]Kenny, 160-161. Muhlenberg believed the Moravian Indians did on occasion attack white settlers, and furthermore believed that the German settlers in the backcountry opposed the Paxton Boy's methods, but understood their frustrations and would likely not help bring the Paxton rangers to justice.

[104]Cavaioli, 79.

> Namely, that of being tried by their Equals in the Neighbourhood where their own, their Acusers and the Witnesses Character and Credit, with the Circumstances of the Fact are best known.[105]

Smith and Gibson further argued that had representation within the Assembly been more equitable, no such bill would ever have had a chance of passing.

The third through seventh grievances dealt directly with the Indian problems on the frontier. They range from requesting that the Quakers no longer be allowed to harbor Indians to demanding that all Indians be driven from settled lands. The 8th grievance however was leveled directly at the Quakers. Smith and Gibson claim that several of the Society of Friends were actively working with Indians against the backcountry men. They specifically claim that a lead Quaker, whose name was ultimately redacted, was acting in a facility similar to that of the governor, making treaties and trade agreements with the Indians.

The idea that the primary motivation of the Paxton Boys' march on Philadelphia was political frustration with the ruling parties is given further credence by the reactions of their opponents. A number of Philadelphia Quakers raised their pens in opposition to the backcountry men who threatened their control of colonial matters. Few of these pamphlets spent much time addressing the actual crime committed by the Paxton Boys, but rather warned of the dangers of a Presbyterian government. The "Piss-brutarians" as one Quaker called the Paxton Boys, were part of "a long line of Scotch Presbyterian rebels who, if given power, would unleash similar violent rebellion on Pennsylvania."[106] The Quakers had reason to be nervous. The argument raised by Smith and Gibson in the

---

[105]Smith, 11.

[106]Brubaker, 69.

Remonstrance resonated with people throughout Pennsylvania. It even gained traction among the disenfranchised within Philadelphia. Most of what the Paxton Boys addressed in the *Remonstrance* was dealt with quickly. Scalp bounties resumed in the summer of 1764,[107] the Assembly unilaterally altered trade agreements with tribes, and although a cursory investigation into the massacres was made, Penn's government never arrested any of the Paxton Boys.[108] John Penn was willing to sacrifice justice for the Indians in order to build support in the backcountry against the Quakers who were seeking a royal government for the colony.[109]

There is at least a surface connection between the motivations of the Paxton Boys and the later American Revolution. If not for Benjamin Franklin's renowned diplomatic skill in handling the gathering storm at Germantown, the march of the Paxton Boys could easily have become the equivalent of Lexington and Concord, sparking a larger Pennsylvania-wide rebellion. The language of the only account actually written by two members of the Paxton Boys seems eerily similar to words that would be written by their opponents 10 years later. The attacks on the Conestoga were criminal, regardless of any possible connection between them and the Delaware. While Benjamin Franklin likely exaggerated the violence of the attack on Conestoga Manor, few people disagree with the

---

[107]Ibid., 143.

[108]Ibid., 107.

[109]There were a number of different government types seen within the various colonies from the first settlement at Jamestown through the commencement of the Revolution. Pennsylvania, like the original Carolina, was a proprietary government. Had the Quakers been successful in their bid for establishment of a Royal Government, the Penn family would have lost all control over the colony. Ultimately the Carolinas were converted to Royal colonies with Granville being the last of the original four proprietor families.

assessment that the Paxton Boys killed women and children in both attacks. It is only in the later march on Philadelphia and the writings of Matthew Smith and James Gibson that we see that these attacks, however brutal, were partly fueled by resentment of a government neglecting its responsibilities to its people. While the neglect was deliberate, rooted in racial and religious prejudices against the Scots-Irish that many eastern Pennsylvanians had brought with them from across the Atlantic, the result was a situation that anticipated, in many ways, the situation that all Americans faced in 1775. The march of the Paxton Boys was in some ways "a primary statement in the war for rights and representation which burgeoned into the Revolution."[110]

---

[110]John Dunbar, *The Paxton Papers* (The Hague: Martinus Nijoff, 1957), 48-50.

CHAPTER 5

THE SOUTH CAROLINA REGULATORS

Chaos in the Backcountry

As Benjamin Franklin delicately defused the anger of the Paxton Boys at Germantown, Pennsylvania, about 650 miles to the southwest, a regiment of South Carolina militia marched into the densely forested backcountry. South Carolina's Acting Governor, William Bull, dispatched the regiment with the intent to provide the backcountry settlers with "some sort of Order and Government which they seem generally at present not sufficiently acquainted with." In an environment very similar to that which faced the Paxton Boys in the early 1760s, the Scots-Irish of the South Carolina backcountry were also facing abject neglect by their colonial government. Just as the Indian attacks on the backcountry during the French and Indian War and Pontiac's Rebellion made it clear to the Scots-Irish of Pennsylvania that they were on their own, The Cherokee War of 1759-1761, and the resulting lawlessness, made it clear to the Scots-Irish of South Carolina that they too were on their own.

The Cherokee War in the Carolina and Virginia backcountries was a result of poor Indian relations during the French and Indian War. The Cherokee offered their services to the Virginians in their effort to defend themselves from routine raids from the Shawnee, but the confused and terrorized Virginians frequently attacked Cherokee war parties, mistaking them for the Shawnee. British military commanders also antagonized the Cherokee by discontinuing the long-standing tradition of providing gifts to the Indians in exchange for their military support. The result was a fractured and discontented Cherokee nation that took out their frustrations on the backcountry inhabitants of Virginia and the Carolinas. Acting Governor Bull's predecessor, William Lyttleton, only worsened the situation when he commenced his own failed military campaign against the Cherokee in western South Carolina in 1759. Lyttleton's campaign succeeded only in unifying the majority of the Cherokee nation against the white settlers; it sent the South Carolina backcountry into a state of chaos that would continue for more than five years.

Figure 2.   Map of South Carolina 1767, before the Regulation

Source: Created by author.

One of the most tragic attacks of the war, from the settler's perspective, was the Cherokee attack on Scots-Irish settlers from the Long Canes, just south of the Saluda River. The majority of the Cherokee attacks targeted settlements close to the Cherokee lands at the foothills of the southern Appalachians. The Long Canes settlers thought they would be safe after leaving their homes that were close to Cherokee country and heading to Augusta, well to the southeast. On 1 February 1760, a large group of mounted Cherokee warriors descended on the settlers just a day or so after they began their trip to Augusta. At least 40 of the settlers were killed or captured; the rest scattered and spread word of the terrible attack.[111] These types of attacks continued for the better part of the year. One small Scots-Irish settlement after another found themselves the targets of Cherokee raiding parties. The settlers initially responded in a way that their ancestors in the North of Ireland were all too familiar with. They began building what became known as "settler's forts,"[112] large dwellings surrounded by timber walls. When the signal was given, all the settlers would retreat from their homes to the settler's fort to wait out the attackers. Often, while the settlers took shelter in these makeshift fortifications, the Cherokee warriors escaped with all of their most valuable possessions. The Cherokee were particularly fond of taking black slaves, horses, and wagons. Somewhat reminiscent of the Paxton Boys' response to Pontiac's rebellion, the settlers created parties of rangers who rode well into Cherokee lands and laid waste to their crops and killed any Indian they could find. These parties of rangers and a regiment of British regulars were ultimately effective against the Cherokee, mostly by razing the Middle Towns that

---

[111]Richard Maxwell Brown, *The South Carolina Regulators* (Cambridge: Belknap Press of Harvard University Press, 1963), 4-5.

[112]Ibid.

provided much of the food for the Cherokee. By March of 1761, the Cherokee realized they were losing what had become an attritional war.[113]

Beyond its obvious destructive impact, The Cherokee War had a significant impact on the social structure of the backcountry in South Carolina. Before the war, the backcountry was sparsely populated, but those who braved the untamed wilderness tended to be industrious and had dreams of expanding beyond subsistence farming and becoming wealthy. Many already had made significant headway toward their goal of wealth. While the Scots-Irish of Pennsylvania and North Carolina had difficulty obtaining slaves and experienced difficulty in obtaining more than an initial plot of land, the South Carolinians had no such problems. Charleston was the undisputed hub of slave importation during the colonial era. While most of these slaves found their ways onto the plantations of the low country, a few ended up in the backcountry, typically by less than legal means.[114] Additionally, settlers in South Carolina were able to acquire several tracts of land for low prices and virtually non-existent quitrent. Moses Kirkland, a particularly industrious Scots-Irishman, managed to acquire over 10,000 acres of land in the backcountry. With large tracts of land, a gristmill, a ferry, and slaves to work them, Moses and many like him were able to cease being poor Irish Protestants and became the first of the backcountry's planter elites. The term "planter elite" when used in reference to backcountry inhabitants must, however, be taken in perspective. The first reliable

---

[113]Ibid., 9.

[114]The Creek and Cherokee were often employed to catch runaway slaves and while the owners of these slaves put up healthy rewards for their return, the landowners in the backcountry would often pay higher prices for them. Even with these higher prices, these runaway slaves were far less expensive than if the backcountry inhabitants were to purchase them from the slave market in Charleston.

record of slave ownership throughout the state of South Carolina was the 1800 United States Federal Census. In 1800 James Mayson, a wealthy landowner and justice of the peace for the Ninety Six area, owned 14 slaves, which was an average number for a backcountry planter. His low country counterparts owned an average of 60-100 slaves. Some of the largest slave-owners, like William Alston of Waccamaw Township, owned over 500.[115] While early backcountry planters like Mayson could never compete with the likes of Alston, they no longer considered themselves poor Scots-Irish settlers trying to eek out a living. The war with the Cherokees threatened to destroy what these men had managed to put together, and they were the ones who contributed most to the backcountry's defense. Mayson was a Captain in the militia and led several operations against the Cherokee. Kirkland was also a Captain in the rangers and while little is known of his activities during the Cherokee War, his later service during the Revolution would indicate that he was likely a very active militia officer.[116]

Other backcountry inhabitants, who had not fared as well or who had arrived more recently, responded in different ways to the violence of the Cherokee War. Many simply chose to leave, seeking safer places in North Carolina and Virginia. Others chose a more nefarious route. With what property they once owned destroyed or stolen during the war, these men resorted to crime in order to subsist. The wealthy planters referred to

---

[115]US Federal Census Year: 1800; Census Place: Waccamaw, Georgetown District, South Carolina; Roll: 49; Page: 379; Image: 27; Family History Library Film: 181424.

[116]Keith Krawczynski, *William Henry Drayton: South Carolina Revolutionary Patriot* (Baton Rouge: Louisiana State University Press, 2001), 159.

these raiders as outlaws and *banditti*.[117] These outlaws took advantage of the chaos during the aftermath of the Cherokee War and roamed the backcountry in armed groups, stealing horses and tormenting those who chose to stay. The majority of both sides of this new social conflict were Scots-Irish. The backcountry of South Carolina was beginning to resemble the lowlands of Scotland just prior to the creation of the Plantation of Ulster. Rather than Border Reivers causing havoc on the border of Scotland and England, the bandits were causing havoc on the South Carolina frontier.

The root causes of the bandit problem were remarkably similar to those that had produced the Border Reivers. Frequent conflict between Scotland and England had resulted in a lawless borderland that was neglected by both the British and the Scottish crowns. In South Carolina, the Cherokee War created the wasteland, but the lawlessness actually predated the conflict. The backcountry of South Carolina was unique in the colonies in that there was no legal infrastructure outside of Charleston. When outlaws were caught in the backcountry, the justice of the peace had to transport the criminal to Charleston and schedule a hearing. Frequently hearings could not be scheduled for several weeks, requiring the justice to return to his home to care for his crops and family. To secure a conviction, several witnesses would be required to testify. It was difficult to convince witnesses to abandon their homestead responsibilities for a prolonged legal endeavor. Often this inefficient process enabled the criminals to escape without ever being brought to trial. In cases of property theft of relatively low value, there was no benefit to be gained by bringing the criminal to trial since the expenses incurred by the

---

[117]Michael C. Scoggins, *The Day It Rained Militia: Huck's Defeat and the Revolution in the South Carolina Backcountry, May-July 1780* (Charleston, SC: History Press, 2005), 20.

100-250 mile trip would simply lead to more loss by the victim.[118] The lack of backcountry courts was identified as a problem for the residents as early as 1721, when the South Carolina Assembly passed an act establishing five precincts tasked with covering the backcountry. Although the act was never repealed, it fell by the wayside as lawyers refused to show up to the courts, and the courts themselves were still far closer to Charleston than to the people they were intended to serve.[119] Further attempts were made in 1741 and 1752 to establish a backcountry legal system, but to no avail. The Assembly decided that it was simply too expensive to establish the courts, so both attempts before even receiving a vote.[120] Generally the executive leaders in the South Carolina Government seemed more apt to support the backcountry requests for courts. Governor James Glen supported the 1752 petition for courts to be established in the back settlements, and in 1764, Lieutenant Governor Bull attempted to deal with the growing problem of the bandits by sending a militia regiment into the backcountry. While militias might have been effective against raiding Indians, law enforcement was somewhat beyond their capacity.[121]

The backcountry residents of South Carolina gave the low country government fair warning of their dissatisfaction over the apathy in Charleston toward their concerns.

---

[118]Brown, *Regulators,* 12-13.

[119]Charles Woodmason and Richard James Hooker, *The Carolina Backcountry on the Eve of the Revolution; The Journal and Other Writings of Charles Woodmason, Anglican Itinerant* (Chapel Hill: Published for the Institute of Early American History and Culture at Williamsburg, VA, by the University of North Carolina Press, 1953), 166-167.

[120]Ibid.

[121]Brown, *Regulators*, 23.

In early 1766 a petition appeared before the Assembly that bore strong resemblance to the *Remonstrance* of the Paxton Boys two years prior. The petition complained about the lack of representation for the backcountry within the Assembly. Other grievances were the lawlessness created by the roving outlaws, and the disproportionate taxes paid by backcountry landowners. The concern over property taxes dealt with the fact that backcountry residents were taxed at the same per-acre rate as their low country counterparts, despite the fact that the backcountry land was less valuable and produced fewer profit-making crops.[122]

The Assembly made little or no attempt to remedy the injustices of representation and taxes, but they did repeatedly attempt to address the issues of lawlessness by finally passing a circuit court act. The Assembly could not act unilaterally, and such drastic changes in colonial law required ratification by the British Parliament, which fought the South Carolina Assembly vehemently.[123] It is uncertain whether the leading men of the backcountry were aware of the Assembly's efforts to address one of their chief grievances, but by 1767 the state of lawlessness within the backcountry became so severe that they took justice into their own frontier hands.

The Regulation

By early August 1767, the law-abiding backcountry settlers decided they were done waiting for the courts in Charleston to regulate the pervasive lawlessness that endangered their lives and property. A large group of men, generally from the area

---

[122] Woodmason and Hooker, 169.

[123] Brown, *Regulators*, 70-72.

between the Broad and Saluda Rivers, gathered in bands and began punishing the outlaws. The punishments doled out by these groups of angered backcountry men can hardly be called "justice" in the technical legal sense. Outlaws were dragged from their homes, their cabins were burned to the ground, and often the outlaws were left naked, tied to trees. In many cases, the vigilantes mercilessly whipped the outlaws until their backs were raw.[124] Instead of frightening other outlaws into obedience, the actions of the vigilantes had the opposite effect. The outlaws fought back, and for many months the backcountry devolved into a violent civil war.

The rage of the outlaws was directed largely at the few lawmen in the backcountry. A backcountry justice of the peace was the closest thing there was to a sheriff. While their authority was limited to temporary arrests and jailing, they were men who garnered considerable respect from the respectable. This position of authority made them targets of the outlaws. The fact that the outlaws targeted these justices is also, perhaps, evidence that these men were among those early vigilantes that punished the outlaws so severely. In the late night hours of 8 October 1767, James Mayson was dragged out of his bed by a band of outlaws and tied to a horse before being forcibly transported eighty miles away, where he was tried by a panel of outlaws, found guilty and punished.[125]

The cycle of ratcheting up the violence continued. Just as the initial vigilante attacks caused an increase in outlaw audacity, the attacks on the justices served only to

---

[124] Rachel Klein, "Ordering the Backcountry: The South Carolina Regulation," *The William and Mary Quarterly* 38, no. 4 (October 1981): 661.

[125] Ibid., 674.

galvanize the resolve of the vigilantes. What had begun as loosely organized bands formed into organized groups resembling militia companies. By late October, the groups assumed the name "Regulators," which would be associated with them for the remainder of their movement. The term has a lengthy history among vigilante groups, dating back to 1688 just prior to the Glorious Revolution in England.[126] The choice of the title is important. It shows that in the eyes of the vigilantes, the violence they committed was acceptable since it served to 'regulate' the unruly members of their backcountry society. Rather than seeing themselves as practitioners of mob-justice, the Regulators saw themselves as performing a right and just function that their government refused to.

Estimates of the Regulator strength in the backcountry vary widely, but conservative estimates put the overall Regulator strength at about 5,000 men.[127] The Regulators were spread thin, since they covered the backcountry from the Peedee River in the east to Ninety-Six in the West. Although 5,000 men was certainly a force large enough to catch the attention of the colonial government, policing the entire backcountry became a full time job for the Regulators.

Many of the outlaws mistakenly assumed that the Regulators would not chase them beyond the confines of South Carolina, but they underestimated the desire of the Regulators to bring order to the backcountry. In December 1767, Thomas Woodward of the southern portion of the Broad River commanded a group of Regulators pursuing some horse thieves who had fled into North Carolina. Woodward's Regulators followed the

---

[126] *Oxford English Dictionary,* 2d ed., s.v. "Regulators" [CD-ROM] (Oxford: Oxford University Press, 1992).

[127] Brown, *Regulators,* 113.

outlaws into North Carolina, trailing them all the way to present-day Mount Airy on the North Carolina-Virginia border. After a short siege, in which the Regulators set a number of cabins on fire, they apprehended the fleeing outlaws and hung sixteen on the spot.

Other Regulators far surpassed Woodward's ranging tendencies, chasing outlaws as far as Augusta and Loudoun Counties, Virginia.[128] Joseph Kirkland, a possible cousin of Moses, ranged just as far but seemed less apt toward violence. In January 1768, he ushered his captives all the way to the jails of Wilmington, North Carolina.

Initially, the colonial government in Charleston was alarmed by the sudden rampant vigilantism in the backcountry. Governor Montague addressed the Assembly on 5 November 1767:

> Hon. Gen[tn]: I should think myself equally negligent in the duty I owe my King and this Province, if I did not recommend to you an early and serious consideration of the unhappy situation of the Back Parts of this Country. The various acts of villainy committed there, in contempt of all laws, human and divine, we have too frequent accounts of, and too recent proofs of, in the late trials of the unhappy convicts now under sentence of death. Far remote from the seat of Justice, they are daily exposed to misery and distress. These are objects that require redress and are worthy the care of the Legislature. Tumultuous risings of any people, if not properly attended to, are of dangerous tendency, and they are a disgrace to a country, and particularly pernicious to a commercial and newly settled colony. The means to suppress those licentious spirits that have so lately appeared in the distant parts of the Province, and, assuming the name of Regulators, have, in defiance of Government, and to the subversion of good order, illegally tried, condemned and punished many persons, require an attentive deliberation.[129]

In retrospect, the words Governor Montague spoke to the assembly, claiming that "[t]umultuous risings of any people" were dangerous and disgraceful seem ironic. Many

---

[128]Ibid., 45.

[129]Alexander Gregg, *History of the Old Cheraws* (New York: Richardson and Co., 1867), 136.

in the Assembly would later be among the most vocal leaders of rebellion in South Carolina. Two days after the Governor addressed the Assembly, they received a visit from "those licentious spirits." Four leading Regulators—Moses Kirkland, Thomas Woodward, Benjamin Hart and John Scott—arrived in Charleston with a document listing their grievances. Weeks earlier, Lieutenant Governor Bull had received word that 4,000 Regulators intended to march on Charleston to make their demands. He communicated through Charles Woodmason, a trusted Anglican minister, that it would be more desirable if the demands could be delivered "in a constitutional way."[130] Once the Assembly and Governor Montague had a chance to review the *Regulator Remonstrance*, they seemed to have had a complete change of heart towards the Regulators. The Assembly authorized two ranger companies to deal with the outlaw problem. Both were put under the command of prominent Regulators, Woodward and Henry Hunter. All the officers of the two companies were also Regulators.[131] Given the earlier failures of militia to deal with the outlaws, it stands to reason that the only effect of the authorization was to deputize the Regulator movement, officially ignoring their extreme forms of justice.

Armed with this legal *carte blanche*, the Regulators guaranteed that the outlaw problem in the backcountry would be short-lived. In a violent campaign from November 1767 to late March 1768, the Regulators beat, burned, hanged, and shot anyone associated with the outlaw gangs. Although the terror of the backcountry outlaws was mostly over by March, the Regulators were not ready to resume their domestic lives. In June a large meeting of leading Regulators was held in The Congarees where they agreed

---

[130]Brown, *Regulators*, 41.

[131]Ibid., 44.

to expand their 'regulation' beyond combating outlaws. Their new mission would be to "purge, by methods of their own, the country of all idle persons, all that have not a visible way of getting an honest living."[132] With order restored to the backcountry, the Regulators seemed intent to construct a social order in which everyone would be productive, and they themselves would be the new elite. A large component of their reformation was the enforcement of Protestant values. Much to Woodmason's chagrin, they were predominantly Presbyterian and Baptist ethics. Woodmason noted that the few Anglican Regulators that there were left for Presbyterian meetinghouses.[133] In his journal, he wrote that while the Presbyterians hated the Baptists, and vice versa, "they will unite altogether—in a Body to distress or injure the Church establish'd."[134] Far more distressing to Governor Montague, they also resolved to ignore any attempts by Charleston to re-establish legal authority over the backcountry. In one short meeting, the Regulators ceased to be men of frontier justice and began to flirt with rebellion.

The regulation of the 'low people,' as the Regulators called them, took a different form than the regulation of the outlaws. The Regulators whipped and drove out the vagrants they viewed as not "reclaimable." But rather than shoot or hang the remaining vagrants, they pressed them into a form of sharecropping. Large backcountry landowners would grant them "so many acres to attend in so many days, on pain of Flagellation."[135]

---

[132]Anthony Pinn, *Terror and Triumph: The Nature of Black Religion* (Minneapolis: Fortress Press, 2003), 59.

[133]Brown, *Regulators*, 59.

[134]Woodmason and Hooker, 43.

[135]Klein, *Ordering the Backcountry*, 678.

The Regulators were intent on creating a society that mirrored much of the rest of the South, in which farming was the basis of all social order.[136] According to Samuel Boykin, a prominent Regulator, those low people who were drawn into this sharecropping system "did work, and lead a better life" despite the occasional whipping that had to be administered. While it would be expected that a Regulator would take this perspective on their activities, there may be a basis in fact for this perspective. Boykin personally tied Bennet Dozier to a tree and administered "39 lashes well laid on." Yet this punishment was administered at the behest of Dozier's wife who told Boykin that her husband was "a slothful individual and poor provider."[137]

Although the government in Charleston was concerned with the severity of the punishment that the Regulators dealt to their enemies, it was their declaration of the Plan of Regulation in June of 1768 that caused a marked change in Charleston's attitude towards the backcountry vigilantes. Their refusal to acknowledge the low country government's authority within the backcountry struck Lieutenant Governor Bull as tantamount to rebellion. He dispatched a constable with warrants of distress for the property of a number of leading Regulators along the Peedee River.[138] The constable prudently brought about a dozen low country militiamen with him to avoid falling into

---

[136]Ibid.

[137]Brown, *Regulators*, 50-51.

[138]Woodmason and Hooker, 175. Warrants of Distress were issued to compel payment for outstanding debts to the government such as quitrents, or other taxes. Since the Regulators were particularly vicious against debtors in the backcountry, it is unlikely that several leading Regulators would have been in debt themselves. It is likelier that the warrants the constable tried to serve were meant more to intimidate the Regulators rather than to actually seize land.

the Regulators' hands; however, in late July, the Regulators surrounded the constable and his militiamen in a clearing at Marr's Bluff. After the two sides exchanged several words, shouting from behind the cover of trees, they began exchanging gunfire. Severely outnumbered, the constable beat a hasty retreat, leaving several of his men to be captured and abused by the Regulators.[139]

Several weeks later, the Colonial Provost Marshall himself, Roger Pinckney, decided to go to Marr's Bluff to serve papers on the defiant Regulators. Well aware of the fate of his constable, Pinckney called upon two Peedee River militia companies to meet him there. Once Pinckney arrived at the home of Gideon Gibson, one of the Regulators he hoped to bring to justice, he saw that the militia was already there. As the Provost approached the militia to confer with their commanders, he discovered that they had brought 300 men rather than the 100 he expected. Furthermore, after his brief conversation with the commanders, he discovered that they were there to protect Gibson, not him. Thankfully for Pinckney, cooler heads prevailed and he was permitted to return to Charleston, empty-handed but unharmed.[140]

For the better part of a year, the Regulators ruled the backcountry virtually independent of Charleston. Although they enforced their own laws and refused to pay taxes, the Regulators did organize a march on low country polling places for the Assembly election in late summer 1768. The organized voting initiative successfully put several backcountry men, themselves Regulators, into the Assembly.[141] The attempt to

---

[139]Brown, *Regulators,* 54-55.

[140]Ibid., 56.

[141]Ibid., 61-62.

gain representation within the colonial assembly indicates that the Regulators perhaps viewed the *de facto* independence of the backcountry as a temporary condition. The excitement from having gained seats in the Assembly did not last long. Governor Montague dissolved the Assembly in November because of their recent public support of Massachusetts against the Townshend acts of 1767.[142]

Just as the Governor dissolved the Assembly, a strong anti-Regulator movement began to coalesce in the backcountry. These anti-Regulators called themselves Moderators, communicating their dissatisfaction by means of the same extreme methods used by the Regulators. In reality, the Moderators consisted largely of former outlaws, led by other members of the backcountry middle class, who resented the growing economic and political power of the Regulators.[143] Using the same ruthless methods of the Regulators, the Moderators fought back. Just as was the case in the early Regulation of the outlaws, the violence between the Regulators and the Moderators quickly escalated to the point that low country militias refused to march into the backcountry to stop the conflict. For several months, the two sides effectively re-fought the initial Regulation that took place in 1767. With the added help of several leading property owners, the Moderators were far more organized and effective than the bands of outlaws had been by themselves.

---

[142]Ibid., 63. The Townshend acts were a series of English parliamentary policies designed to enforce revenue acts in the colonies. The Stamp Act of 1765 had been largely a failure since it was difficult to enforce. Many colonies felt the Townshend Acts were heavy handed and unconstitutional.

[143]Ibid., 91-92.

On 23 March 1769, the two met in their largest engagement. Almost a thousand men from each side met for battle at the confluence of the Saluda and Bush Rivers in present-day Newberry County. Despite the apparent readiness of both sides for a bloodbath, three respected men who had abstained from Regulator or Moderator activities appeared and persuaded both sides to stand down. Richard Richardson, William Thomson, and Daniel McGirt ultimately got both sides to agree to cease all operations and let the law of the land re-assert itself in the backcountry. After nine years of almost constant violence, it appeared at last as if the backcountry had fought itself into exhaustion.

Figure 3. Map of South Carolina 1770, after the Regulation

Source: Created by author.

Before the year was out, Lieutenant Governor Bull announced the passage of the Circuit Court Act of 1769. The act established a legal structure for the backcountry, effectively addressing one of the Regulator's chief complaints.[144] The problem of under representation of the backcountry continued, and occasionally Regulator activity still occurred in the years leading up to the Revolution, but these activities were infrequent and localized. With their chief concerns resolved, the Regulators were never again able to organize widespread resistance.[145]

Motivating the Regulation

With the exception of a few of the leading Regulators, little is known about the 5,000 or so men who comprised the movement. After the truce between the Moderators and Regulators, Governor Montague pardoned a large number of Regulators by name; however, the only pardons that remain within the South Carolina Archives are for 118 men who lived between the Broad and Wateree Rivers. Of the 118 men listed in the available pardons, 48 were accompanied by many of their close family. Moses Kirkland was only one of five Kirkland men from the area who assisted in the regulation, and James Andrews Sr. from Morrison's Creek along the Little River brought his two sons, James Jr. and Enoch into the effort. In addition to the familial aspect of the movement, the Regulators that were pardoned by the Governor also shared a socio-economic status. Few of the 118 leading men owned less than 100 acres, the standard head right, while most owned in excess of 300 acres. Many were slave owners, some owning as many as

---

[144] Woodmason and Hooker, 184-185.

[145] Brown, *Regulators,* 95.

30 slaves.[146] Some like Richard Maxwell Brown and Rachel Klein have placed much significance on the socio-economic divide between the Regulators and the outlaws and vagrants. These two historians have framed the Regulation as a struggle between the "haves" and the "have nots." While there is certainly a significant economic component to the regulation, land and slave records for South Carolina suggest that the advanced socio-economic status of the known Regulators may have been unique to those leading Regulators who later received gubernatorial pardons. Of the roughly 80,000 slaves who lived in South Carolina in the mid 1760s, about 1/12th were owned by backcountry farmers.[147] This would place just less than 6,700 slaves in the backcountry. The 118 named Regulators account for 594 of these 6,700 backcountry slaves.[148] If the rate of slave ownership were consistent across the 5,000-man strong Regulator movement, over 23,000 slaves would have lived in the backcountry rather than 6,700. It is possible that those lesser Regulators who bore the brunt of the Regulation looked at these leading men as examples of what they too might one day have if they could bring order to the backcountry.

All of this is to say that the Regulators were undoubtedly motivated to some degree by their familial and economic ties to the backcountry. They were farmers who were either on the verge of expanding beyond subsistence farming or were firmly within an early manifestation of the southern backcountry planter elites. Their foes: outlaw,

---

[146]Brown, *Regulators,* 145.

[147]Rachel Klein, *Unification of a Slave State: The Rise of the Planter Class in the South Carolina Backcountry, 1760-1808* (Chapel Hill: University of North Carolina Press, 1990), 151.

[148]Brown, *Regulators*, 145-148.

vagrant, and Moderator alike, were mostly other backcountry Scots-Irishmen, and many Moderators were wealthy farmers who owned many slaves.[149] Thus, there may have been a considerable clan-conflict component to the struggle in addition to the ethno-cultural and economic components.

The full set of motivations that drove the Regulators to clash headlong with both their kinsmen and their colonial government are complex and important; however, those complaints that were communicated to the Assembly in November 1767 provide an important anticipation of the later revolution.

The *Remonstrance* delivered by Kirkland, Hunter, Hart, and Scott on 7 November 1767 remains the best glimpse into the attitudes behind the Regulation. Although Woodmason, the itinerant Anglican minister, penned it, much of the document reads as an authentic plea for increased government involvement in the backcountry. The lengthy document can generally be broken down into seven key complaints. Primarily, the backcountry settlers were concerned with the abject lack of law and order, which created the problem with the outlaws. They were frustrated by the fact that their lands were taxed at the same rate as the low country plantations, even though their lands produced far less profit. They felt as if there was little hope for change in their situation since they had communicated their complaints several times previously to no avail. Exorbitantly high fees charged by lawyers and low country courts hindered backcountry business, and when charged with crimes, they were not tried by their peers but rather by low country planters.[150] This last complaint seems ironic given the ruthlessness with

---

[149]Klein, *Ordering the Backcountry*, 678.

[150]Woodmason and Hooker, 213-220.

which the Regulators administered their own brand of law in the backcountry. Few outlaws were given the benefit of a trial at all, much less a trial of their peers.

The final grievance communicated in the body of the *Remonstrance* was the under representation of the backcountry within the South Carolina House of Commons. Woodmason notes that while the low country inhabitants elected forty-four members of the Assembly, those from the backcountry accounted for merely six.[151] Many of the complaints Woodmason communicates on this matter seem significantly linked to the same complaints made by New England radicals a decade later.

> From this our Non-Representation in the House, We conceive it is; That Sixty thousand Pounds Public Money, (of which we must pay the Greater Part, as being levy'd on the Consumer) hath lately been voted, for to build an *Exchange* for the Merchants, and a *Ball-Room* for the Ladies of Charlestown; while near *Sixty thousand* of Us Back Settlers, have not a Minister, or a place of Worship to repair too![152]

Woodmason was likely the source for the additional comment about lacking ministers and places of worship. The backcountry was not short of places to worship, or short of ministers. Many Baptist and Presbyterian meetinghouses littered the backcountry, and itinerants from Pennsylvania and Virginia frequently traveled through the area by Woodmason's own admission in his journal.[153] Nevertheless, ever the Anglican, Woodmason could not avoid the chance to campaign for additional funds for the conversion of backcountry radical Protestants.

---

[151] Ibid., 221.

[152] Ibid.

[153] Ibid., 42 and 74.

While the concern over lack of representation may at first seem to be tacked on to the end of a long list of other complaints, Woodmason properly identifies this single grievance as the likely cause of all the others. "It is to this Great Disproportion of Representatives on our Part, that our Interests have been so long neglected, and the Back Country disregarded."[154] In a foreshadowing of an argument that would later pre-occupy the constitutional conventions, he remarked, "it is the Number of *Free Men*, not *Black Slaves*, that constitute the Strength and Riches of a State."[155]

Additional links between the South Carolina Regulation and the later revolution are evident in a somewhat unlikely source. Unbeknownst to the Regulators themselves, the South Carolina Assembly had taken up the Regulators' cause in 1767. The Assembly drafted the Circuit Court Act of 1768 as a means of furthering their own grievances against the Crown. The central issue that the low country politicians sought to leverage was the status of South Carolina judicial tenure.[156] While judges in England had been serving unlimited tenures based on "good behavior" since the Glorious Revolution, judges in the colonies were subject to tenures of the King's pleasure.[157] Thomas Jefferson would later list judicial tenure as one of the "repeated injuries" which "made it necessary for one people to dissolve the political bands which have connected them with another."

---

[154]Ibid., 221.

[155]Ibid.

[156]Brown, *Regulators*, 65.

[157]Joseph Tiedemann, *Reluctant Revolutionaries: New York City and the Road to Independence, 1763-1776* (Ithaca: Cornell University Press, 2008), 52. Tenure of good behavior was essentially a lifetime appointment, similar to current federal justices. Barring serious criminal conviction, the judges would serve for life or until retirement. The tenure of King's pleasure on the other hand placed the judge's position in a precarious position of easily being removed by royal decree.

He addressed the issue directly in the *Declaration of Independence*, citing: "He has made Judges dependent on his Will alone, for the tenure of their offices, and the amount and payment of their salaries."[158]

The most crucial aspect of the Circuit Court Act of 1768 that prevented its ratification by the British Parliament was its demand that South Carolina judges be appointed for tenures based on good behavior. Although Parliament acknowledged that the existing situation in the backcountry prevented further settlement, and full economic development, they recoiled at the bill's demand the appointment of judges for tenures of good behavior.[159] Ultimately, Parliament rejected the act, and the South Carolina Assembly was faced with the realization that in order to extend the benefit of judicial infrastructure to the backcountry, they would have to concede on the issue of judicial tenure. In the later Circuit Court Act of 1769, the Assembly submitted to Parliament what might today be called a "clean bill," with no mention of altering the existing fundamental arrangements.[160]

It seems strange that the Regulators of South Carolina resorted to extra-legal actions in order to bring legal infrastructure to the backcountry. The Plan of Regulation that they agreed to in early 1768 seemed as if it might be the prelude to a secession movement, yet the Regulators continued to participate in colonial elections. It must be remembered however, that the majority of those whom we consider our founding fathers

---

[158]Thomas Fleming, *A Disease in the Public Mind: A New Understanding of Why We Fought the Civil War* (New York: Da Capo Press, 2013), 31.

[159]Brown, *Regulators*, 79.

[160]Ibid., 101.

remained proponents of reconciliation with the Crown up to the Battle of Bunker Hill. A month before the battle, John Dickenson led the drafting of the Olive Branch Petition; an attempt to appeal to the King's sense of benevolence. Although some in the Continental Congress felt the effort was in vain, Thomas Jefferson commenced the writing of the petition, and even firebrands like Samuel Adams signed it.[161] In the case of the American Revolution, Lord North's parliament and the young King George III refused any effort at reconciliation, continuously antagonizing the colonials. Were it not for the concessions made in the Circuit Court Act of 1769, the Regulators of South Carolina may very well have continued their rebellion to the point of seeking independence.

---

[161]Michael Waller, *Founding Political Warfare Documents of the United States* (Washington, DC: Crossbow Press, 2009), 226.

CHAPTER 6

THE NORTH CAROLINA REGULATORS

Arbitrary Tyranny

Although historians have frequently compared the Regulator movements of North and South Carolina, there was little in common between the movements beyond the name, and perhaps the desire to be seen as the righteous side of the conflict. Despite the differences in the causes and outcomes of the two Regulator movements, the demographics of the two movements were similar. The South Carolina Regulators were predominantly Scots-Irish Presbyterians and Baptist farmers who either had aspirations of wealth, or had already achieved wealth in the backcountry. This profile of the South Carolina Regulators could easily apply to the North Carolina Regulators with a few adjustments. Although Presbyterianism was the predominant faith of the backcountry, Separate Baptist sects actually dominated among the Regulators in North Carolina.[162] Beyond that marginal difference, the two movements had very similar demographics.

The prologue, and causes of the North Carolina Regulation were very different from those to their south. The French and Indian War, which caused so much havoc in Pennsylvania and South Carolina, did not entirely spare North Carolina; however, the conflict did a great deal to populate the colony's backcountry. Many frontier settlers in Pennsylvania and Virginia who found themselves victims of Indian raids fled to the

---

[162] Carole Watterson Troxler, *Farming Dissenters: The Regulator Movement in Piedmont North Carolina* (Raleigh, NC: Office of Archives and History, North Carolina Department of Cultural Resources, 2011), 152.

relative safety of the Piedmont of North Carolina.[163] The Piedmont was attractive to the settlers because inexpensive Crown land was available, and vast swaths of land were still owned by the descendant of one of the original proprietors, Lord John Carteret, 2nd Earl Granville.

The colonies of North and South Carolina had been a single colony from 1663 to 1729. Originally a proprietary colony like Pennsylvania, Carolina was divided among eight English noblemen who generally neglected their possessions, or simply treated them as an economic venture. The eight Lords Proprietors and their agents rarely agreed on how the vast colony should be administered or defended, which led to a dysfunctional government. In 1729, seven of the frustrated Lords Proprietors sold their interests in the colony back to the Crown and the Colony was split into two royal colonies. The eighth Lord Proprietor, Granville, refused to sell his interest to the Crown, retaining ownership of approximately one eighth of North Carolina.[164] Despite their major economic involvement in the development of North Carolina, the Carteret family administered the Granville tract *in absentia.* Earl Granville depended on several agents to handle the daily administration of the vast swaths of land. These agents cheated Granville and the settlers who sought land within the tract. Through their close relationships with local officials, Granville's land agents ran roughshod over the backcountry settlers throughout the mid eighteenth-century.[165]

---

[163]Ibid., 3.

[164]Ibid., 2.

[165]Ibid., 8, 12, 33, 47.

The system of government in North Carolina was a virtually impenetrable old-boy network that, within the backcountry, resembled an organized crime syndicate. Officials at each level of government had a stake in supporting the level above, and the highest-level officials had a stake in keeping the local officials happy. The Governor appointed local Justices of the Peace based on the approval of the lower house of the assembly. The Justices then recommended their friends and business partners for the posts of sheriff, clerk of deeds, or other lucrative local positions. Additionally, there was no law against holding multiple offices, so the potential existed for all local power to be vested in a handful of men. Completing the circle of power, these local power brokers ran the elections in which taxpaying males elected representatives within the House of Commons. In some cases, votes in these elections were cast verbally in a board of inquiry fashion. This flagrant voter intimidation ensured that whatever person the local power holders supported was always elected to the legislature.[166]

The purpose of this closed circle of power was not simply to wield arbitrary authority over the settlers of the colony; public positions, although frequently non-paid, were highly lucrative forms of employment. Because sheriffs and clerks of court and deeds were unpaid positions, they were expected to survive on the fees they charged for their services. Sheriffs appointed the monthly juries, and legislators depended on the local political authorities for their support, so in effect, there were no restrictions on what these

---

[166]Ibid., 11.

local officials could charge.[167] This abuse by fee was compounded by the fact that money in specie or notes was quite scarce in the backcountry.[168]

There was widespread wealth in the backcountry, but the wealth was in the form of land ownership, livestock, crops, and whiskey. These more tangible forms of wealth were not acceptable for paying the court fees demanded by local magistrates. The resulting inability to pay court fees constituted a very real legal liability. This awkward circumstance placed otherwise wealthy farmers in debt to their local magistrates, who added insult to injury by having the farmers work off this debt by working the magistrate's lands instead of their own. Such a system damaged the farmers' ability to tend their own crops, making it necessary for them to incur even more debt to support their families. This inevitably started a vicious cycle that ruined more than one farmer who, until having confrontations with the local sheriff, had considered himself wealthy.[169]

Land agents of major landowners added to the misery of backcountry Scots-Irish settlers, using their close connections with local officials to push recently arrived settlers off their lands in much the same way that Indians were displaced from their lands further north. Land purchasing procedures within the backcountry were admittedly confusing, providing ample opportunity for the land agents to exploit this confusion. Settlers who

---

[167]Marjoleine Kars, *Breaking Loose Together The Regulator Rebellion in Pre-Revolutionary North Carolina* (Chapel Hill: University of North Carolina Press, 2002), 136.

[168]Ibid., 51.

[169]Mary Medley, *History of Anson County, North Carolina, 1750-1976* (Wadesboro, NC: Anson County Historical Society, 1976), 30-31.

believed that they were residing on lawfully purchased Crown land would often receive unwelcome visits from land agents of wealthy major landowners, to find that they were in fact on someone else's land. Others, who purchased their land from these land agents, were later told that they had not completed the legal title process, therefore invalidating their claim on the land.[170] Farmers faced with this set of circumstances were forced to choose one of three options: pay again for their land, including paying for the value of any improvements they made, surrendering their land to these land agents, or resisting through whatever means they had. Given the monetary problems of the backcountry, few settlers had the means to pay for their land plus the value of their improvements. Many ended up losing their land to the land agents who in turn sold these lands to local officials for a fraction of their value.[171]

Many others chose resistance. Organized but largely peaceful resistance to local authorities was something of a backcountry pastime in mid eighteenth-century North Carolina. Although threats of violence occasionally were made, rarely did large-scale violence occur. Sometimes the objects of backcountry frustration might be be hogtied and carried out of the county.[172] The earliest large-scale civil disobedience of local authorities in the backcountry occurred in late 1758. A number of Scots-Irish farmers from Edgecombe, Halifax, and Granville counties petitioned the legislature to investigate the unethical practices of Granville's land agents. Although the legislature acknowledged that land fraud was occurring widely in the backcountry, they absolved Granville's chief

---

[170]Kars, 27.

[171]Troxler, 7.

[172]Ibid., 9.

land agent, Francis Corbin, of any wrongdoing.[173] Frustrated by the lack of results produced by lawful petition, the farmers kidnapped Corbin and forced him to open his bookkeeping for public examination.[174] Once Corbin's books were examined, they revealed that he was charging far more in fees than Earl Granville authorized. Granville fired Corbin and replaced him, but the practices of fee gauging and land stealing continued throughout the 1760s.

The high water mark of violence prior to the Regulation occurred in mid 1765. Scots-Irish settlers in Mecklenberg County, the far western frontier of North Carolina, thought they had settled well beyond any of the large claims in the central Piedmont. In 1761, Henry McCulloh, the son of a large landowner whose claims frequently conflicted with Granville's, rode into Mecklenberg County and informed these settlers that they were squatting on his father's land.[175] McCulloh's first visits to the backcountry were not well received. Although he offered these settlers decent terms, most felt that having to pay for improvements to the land that their own labor created was excessive. He returned in late 1764, hoping to gain traction by bringing the law with him. McCulloh negotiated with a trusted backcountry gentleman named Thomas Polk, the great-uncle of President James Polk, and grandfather of Confederate Lieutenant General Leonidas Polk.[176] While

---

[173]Robert Kumamoto, *The Historical Origins of Terrorism in America: 1644-1880* (New York: Routledge, 2014), 44-45.

[174]Troxler, 8.

[175]Scott Syfert, *The First American Declaration of Independence? The Disputed History of the Mecklenburg Declaration of May 20, 1775* (Jefferson: McFarland and Company, 2013), 41.

[176]James Polk and Milo Milton Quaife, *The Diary of James K. Polk During His Presidency, 1845-1849* (Chicago: McClurg, 1910), xxiii.

McCulloh thought he had struck a deal with Polk, when he returned in late February 1765, a crowd behaving "more like Wolves than rational Beings" greeted him, and Polk was at the head.[177] Polk's men stalked McCulloh day and night, watching over his cabin as he slept, and greeting him in the morning, guns in hand. McCulloh got the message and fled for his life.

A month later, McCulloh sent several surveyors in his stead to lay out plots anyway. The Mecklenberg settlers were through with simple intimidation. A number of men painted themselves black and ambushed the surveyors, severely beating them. One surveyor received such a beating that he "very nearly had daylight let into his skull."[178] After the North Carolina Governor, William Tryon, became involved, a compromise was reached between McCulloh and the 'black boys' of Mecklenberg. The settlers paid McCulloh for his land, but far less than he desired, and they paid nothing for the improvements that they themselves had made.[179] With a compromise reached, the so-called "Sugar Creek War" of 1765 was over, but the conflict in Mecklenberg was a startling move toward violent civil disobedience in the backcountry.

Perhaps in response to the Sugar Creek War, schoolteacher George Sims took to the town square in the community of Nutbush in Granville County. In his ensuing speech to his fellow settlers, Simms essentially urged them to declare independence from those

---

[177] Syfert, 42.

[178] Ibid.

[179] Kars, 47-48.

who attempted to impose "arbitrary tyranny" on them.[180] Sims' argument was inherently dangerous to a government that did not feel accountable to the people it purported to represent. After detailing all the ways in which local officials took advantage of backcountry farmers, Sims declared,

> The Clerks tell us their is no law to ascertain their fees, and therefore they are at liberty to tax our bills as they please, and the misfortune is Gentlemen, that we are obliged to pay it, be it what it may; I think, Gentlemen, if there be no law to ascertain the Clerk's fees, there is no law to compel us to pay any fees at all.[181]

Sims was not simply a civic-minded schoolteacher, intent on opposing oppressive local government. The language of his conclusion reveals his real motivations. While he argued several times for nonviolent resistance through political petitions, his final words were undoubtedly chosen to excite men to action that might result in their death. When speaking about a potential leader for the movement, Sims said,

> I will be the first on his list to follow him through fire and water, life and death if it be required in defence of my privileges, and if you choose me for your leader I can do no more. Here I am this day with my life in my hand, to see my fellow subjects animated with a spirit of liberty and freedom, and to see them lay a foundation for the recovery thereof, and the clearing our County from arbitrary tyranny.[182]

The immediate reactions to Sims' speech in Nutbush are unknown; however, years later, a new group of men took up the transcript of his speech as their own declaration.

---

[180]North Carolina History, "Petition of Reuben Searcy and Others and an Address to the People of Granville County," http://www.northcarolinahistory.org/encyclopedia/535/entry/ (accessed 9 March 2014).

[181]Ibid.

[182]Ibid.

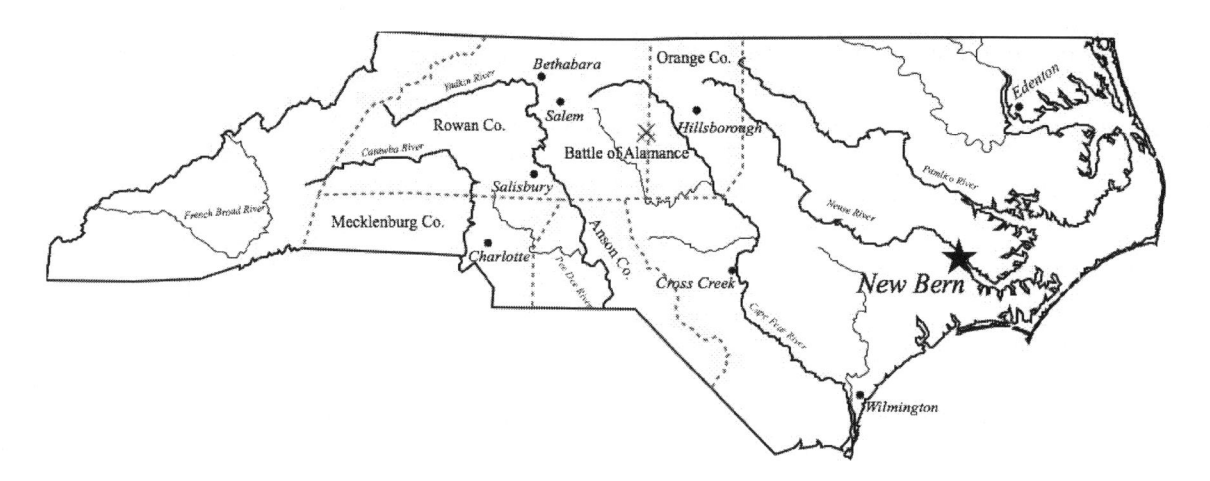

Figure 4. Map of North Carolina in 1765, with select backcountry counties depicted
Source: Created by author.

Relief, by Peaceful Means

Episodes such as the Sugar Creek War, or Sims' public demonstration of discontent at Nutbush were not without precedent. Whig tradition held that government, as it pertained to the people's representatives, was a contract. As historian Marjoleine Kars summarizes the contract, it "rested on the notion that the people could protect their liberties by transferring part of their power and sovereignty to government and abiding by that same government's just laws." The duty of the government within such a contract is to govern through just laws, while the duty of the people is to obey just laws. The problem with such a contract arises when the government no longer governs through just laws. Whig thought held that in such a scenario, the people were duty bound to protest by peaceful means. Petitions, pamphlet writing, and public demonstrations were all largely acceptable and expected forms of peaceful resistance to perceived oppression.[183] Should

---

[183]Kars, 133.

peaceful resistance not achieve the desired resolution, Radical Whigs felt that the people, as the genesis of governmental power, had the right to revolution.[184]

By mid 1766, revolution was not yet on the minds of the farmers of Orange County, still enduring the abuse of local leaders. Most backcountry farmers felt convinced that if they could only communicate their issues to colonial leaders, they could break the stranglehold that local officials had on them.[185] A month after George Sims delivered his Nutbush Address, a group of Separate Baptists along Sandy Creek, collectively called the Sandy Creek Baptist Association, encouraged backcountry farmers to elect representatives for a backcountry congress. This congress met along Sandy Creek to discuss their collective grievances and eventually invited their county leaders to communicate these grievances: in hopes of forcing them to address these grievances, or at least to intimidate them with their own numbers and resolve.[186]

By September, the Sandy Creek Associators felt strong enough to invite their local leaders and Thomas Lloyd, their assemblyman. The main source of trouble for the backcountry farmers of Orange County was Edmund Fanning, one of the most powerful of the backcountry local officials. Fanning was simultaneously holding the offices of assemblyman, register of deeds, militia colonel, and judge of the superior court of Salisbury.[187] On 10 October, the day of the designated meeting between the Sandy Creek Associators and their leaders, Fanning was absent. Instead, the Orange County clerk of

---

[184]Maier, 27-28.

[185]Kars, 134-135.

[186]Ibid., 135.

[187]Ibid.

court arrived, with a message. Fanning, who originally had agreed to meet with the farmers, felt that the language in their invitation suggested that their "congress" was claiming authority it did not possess, and in fact that the farmers' congress constituted an insurrection.[188]

Rather than respond with indignation at the accusation that their gathering constituted an insurrection, the Sandy Creek Associators instead drafted a response and gave it to the clerk of court to take to Fanning. Their response apologized for the confusion that the language of their invitation caused and volunteered to meet Fanning at the Orange County courthouse in Hillsborough.[189] It took the better part of a year for the farmers to raise the money required for a true test of their grievances at court. In August of 1767, several Associators brought their case to the Orange County court. Rather than successfully having their grievances heard, they were laughed out of the court by the judges.[190]

By the end of 1767 and into the beginning of 1768, the movement that started with George Sims and the Sandy Creek Association had expanded well beyond Orange County. Anson, Rowan and Mecklenberg counties all saw an increase in peaceful disobedience of local authority. Herman Husband, one of the leading men of the Sandy Creek Association saw danger in the provocative and threatening language emanating from the neighboring counties. Husband was determined to lead a peaceful, lawful resistance. The men who resisted local sheriffs and tax collectors came to be known as

---

[188]Ibid., 136.

[189]Ibid.

[190]Ibid., 137.

'The Mob' by county officials. Herman suggested that they adopt the title 'Regulator' both to counter the narrative of lawlessness and to encourage the members of the movement to restrain themselves to peaceful resistance.[191]

Husband should not be regarded as a formal leader of the Regulation. While he was well respected by most Regulators, and while he was a leading man within the Sandy Creek Association, the North Carolina Regulation was less cohesive and organized than the South Carolina Regulation. Husband, if anything, was more of a spiritual or ideological leader who shaped the ideas of multiple groups that participated in the Regulation. His control over the conceptual framework that guided the Regulation was tenuous, and it did not take long for many within the Regulation to conclude that their peaceful resistance had failed. Some insisted, evidently guided by Radical Whig thought, that the time for peaceful protest was ending.[192]

Rising Resentment

In late April 1768, a group of about 40 armed Regulators arrived at the Hillsborough court. Their march on the Orange County courthouse was precipitated by the county sheriff's seizure of a prominent Regulator's horse. The Regulator was headed to Hillsborough on business when the sheriff's men detained him on a charge of unpaid taxes. When the Regulator indicated that he could not pay, the sheriff's men took the horse out from under him.[193] The 40 Regulators marched on Hillsborough intent on

---

[191]Ibid., 138.

[192]Troxler, 41-58. For more information on Herman Husband's sometimes confusing influence on the Regulation, see Chapter 4 of Troxler's *Farming Dissenters*.

[193]Kars, 139.

retrieving the horse; but once they arrived, their actions were hardly restricted to horse repossession. They evicted judges and lawyers from the court, and decided to hold their own mock court. Others chose to take out their frustrations on Fanning's home, shooting out the glass in two windows.[194] In response to the April Hillsborough riots, Fanning rode down to Sandy Creek and arrested Husband and William Butler, another man he believed was a leading figure among the Regulators.

The relatively peaceful way in which the Regulators had resisted corrupt local officials began to shift with the arrest of Husband and Butler. Husband and Butler were released, pending trial in the September court session, likely because over 1,000 Regulators had gathered in a camp near Hillsborough, intimidating Fanning.[195] The embattled local justice called on his friend and North Carolina governor, William Tryon. Although Tryon received a letter of petition from the Regulators shortly after the release of Husband and Butler, he sympathized with Fanning, likely at least partly because of an ingrained distaste for the backcountry Scots-Irish. Tryon was also staunchly loyal to the British Crown, and had locked horns with the colonial assembly over their support of Stamp Act resistance. He undoubtedly interpreted the Regulation from the lens of a Crown official fearing a growingly rebellious colony.[196]

Tryon raised a militia force in opposition to the expanding Regulator movement. Unable to effectually press men into service, he relied on volunteers. This made recruiting difficult in the backcountry. Men from Orange, Anson, Rowan, and

---

[194]Ibid., 139-140.

[195]Ibid., 146.

[196]Troxler, 84.

Mecklenburg counties largely supported the Regulator cause. Through enticements of money, and through the recruitment of powerful backcountry leaders like Thomas Polk, Tryon was able to build a large enough militia to intimidate the Regulators.[197] In the months that led up to the Orange County September court session, the Regulators, although pressed by Tryon's growing forces, did some recruiting of their own. While Tryon managed to piece together a force of 1,400 militiamen[198] for the defense of Hillsborough during the court session, over 3,700 Regulators arrived near the end of the second week of September 1768.[199] Many within Hillsborough feared than an armed conflict between the Governor's forces and the Regulators was eminent; however, not a single skirmish occurred between the two forces. The two opposing forces had more influence on the outcome of the September court's proceedings than either had on the other. The court convicted Edmond Fanning of charging fees in excess of what was authorized, and Husband was exonerated of any wrongdoing. Butler was convicted and sentenced to six months in jail, but the Regulators felt vindicated after Governor Tryon pardoned all the Regulators several weeks later.[200]

---

[197]Ibid., 153-156.

[198]Tryon had great difficulty in recruiting backcountry militiamen to his force. Although most of the militia companies of Rowan and Mecklenburg counties offered their support for the Governor, he was only able to raise 147 privates from Rowan and about 300 from Mecklenburg. This would indicate that the majority of men in his 1,400-man force in Hillsborough were from counties well to the East; Kars, 156.

[199]John Alden and Wendell Stephenson, *The South in the Revolution: 1763 - 1789* (Baton Rouge, LA: Louisiana State University Press, 1976), 157-158.

[200]Troxler, 75.

The Orange County September court session was replicated to a lesser extent in several other backcountry counties. The small victory represented by the conviction of Edmond Fanning[201] gave some of the Regulators hope that their concerns could still be addressed peacefully. Much to their dismay, however, officials in other counties successfully delayed and disrupted Regulator lawsuits with administrative obstacles.[202] Rather than discourage the Regulation, the obvious corruption of the backcountry legal system had the opposite effect. The repeated injustices highlighted how widespread and severe the problems were. One Regulator leader wrote that most backcountry farmers "were now fully become sensible of their Oppression, to see themselves thus debarr'd of Justice, and pass unnoticed, when groaning under the weight of their Oppressions."[203] The Regulators were getting stronger.

During this same time, the colonial assembly met in session to deal with a number of issues, some of which directly related to Regulator concerns. Most legislators were economically tied to the circular system of power that gave rise to most of the Regulator complaints, and ultimately they only drafted token legislation to deal with the symptoms of the issue rather than the causes. The only real attempt the legislators made to placate the Regulators' concerns was a limitation on the depreciation of property seized for the payment of public debts.[204] It was a common practice in the backcountry for a sheriff to

---

[201] The conviction of Fanning was indeed a small victory. He was cleared of any malicious wrongdoing, but convicted only of executing a misinterpretation of the law and charged one penny for each count.

[202] Kars, 161.

[203] Ibid., 170.

[204] Ibid., 166.

seize a debtor's property and sell it to a friend for a small fraction of the real value, often leaving the debtor in debt. The 1768 session of the assembly amended an existing law to require multiple officials and at least one freeholder to assess the value of the seized property, and to require the property to be sold at no less than two thirds the established value.[205]

The minor concessions made by the assembly of 1768 did little to meet the concerns of the Regulators. Unlike the major concessions made by South Carolina to quell their Regulator unrest, those made by the North Carolina Assembly had little impact on the Regulation. An opportunity for the Regulators arose in mid 1769 when Governor Tryon dissolved the assembly in retaliation for their resolutions defying the Townshend Acts.[206] Although Tryon understood the danger of holding elections during the Regulation, he must have felt that hanging on to an openly defiant assembly was more dangerous. The backcountry farmers seized the opportunity and elected a number of Regulators to serve as their representatives. Fittingly, Fanning was defeated in his run for reelection by Husband, the long-time supporter of the Regulator cause. The Regulator representatives showed considerable political sophistication, banding together immediately and drafting resolutions that, if adopted into law, would more closely address the root causes of their troubles.[207] Unfortunately, the Regulator representatives were still a small minority of the assembly, and the body had its mind set to displaying

---

[205] Ibid.

[206] Hon. William Williamson, "Laws and Lawyers," *Quarterly Register and Journal of the American Education Society* 15, no. 1 (August 1843): 405-407.

[207] Kars, 172-173.

their growing dissatisfaction with England. Tryon once again dissolved the assembly in November 1769 before any of the resolutions drafted by the Regulator representatives could be voted on.[208]

Right to Rebellion

The insistence of Regulator leaders on non-violent legal resistance to corrupt local leaders was based on their understanding of the English constitution's function as the contract between the governors and the governed. By the beginning of 1770, most backcountry farmers concluded that the constitution was either not in force in North Carolina, or was only protecting the elite.[209] Farmers spent a good deal of early to mid 1770 wrestling with their fields. The 1769 drought, unseasonably cold winter, and heavy spring rainfall pushed the planting of crops later than usual, keeping farmers occupied with their own livelihoods. By fall, fields were planted and the Regulation continued. Regulators sought to continue their legal challenges to corrupt officials, but the September 1770 court session in Orange County proved to be the breaking point for legal recourse.

At the opening of the September session, Justice Richard Henderson announced that he would not allow any Regulator causes to be heard, and threw out a group of Regulators gathered in the courthouse. The resulting riot made the riot of 1768 seem minor in comparison. Clerks and lawyers, including Edmund Fanning, were dragged out of the court and beaten severely. Regulators tore down Fanning's house and destroyed

---

[208]Ibid., 174.

[209]Ibid., 179.

much of his personal belongings. Had it not been for levelheaded leaders, they would have torn down St. Matthew's Anglican Church, the preferred church of the county officials.[210] Most of the lawyers, and more importantly, the judge, fled Hillsborough for the colonial capital at New Bern. Once word of the riot got to Governor Tryon, he decided to pursue two objectives; he requested authorization for a military campaign into the backcountry, and he arrested the recently re-elected Husband for suspicion of supporting the riots.[211] In addition to expelling Husband from the assembly, legislators passed a draconian new riot act, which would make outlaws of anyone participating in a riot.[212] It was passed with retroactive powers, essentially turning the Orange County Regulators into outlaws.[213]

Before adjourning, Legislators approved Tryon's request for funding of a military expedition, but by the time funding was coordinated, it was too late in the year to start a military campaign. In addition to the difficulties of winter campaigning, Tryon had to contend with the difficulty of assembling a force willing to counter the Regulators. Regulator recruiting vastly outpaced Tryon's efforts. By the winter of 1770, large groups of men using the Regulator moniker assembled as far south as Cross Creek, present-day Fayetteville. Even militia musters in New Bern troubled Tryon as many militiamen

---

[210] Troxler, 86-88.

[211] Ibid., 95.

[212] Ibid.

[213] The term outlaw is used here in the eighteenth-century sense. To be declared outlawed was not so much a statement of past criminal activity as it was a true change in legal status. Outlaws were not protected by the law and were therefore subject to being killed without warning, or captured by anyone. The practice of outlawing criminals declined as the capacity for true law enforcement extended into the frontier.

voiced their resolve not to not march against the Regulators.[214] In order to raise a sufficient force, Tryon resorted to offering bonuses of £2 and even drafted men from counties that did not meet their 50-man levy. The draft was exceedingly unpopular among Americans since their strong militia tradition was also a tradition of volunteerism. Many of Tryon's forces were not highly motivated or dedicated to the task. Tryon's musters in the backcountry were met with open defiance. In a muster at newly created Wake County, only 22 men volunteered for the expedition, and more than three-quarters reported to the muster without their weapons, a fineable offense.[215] With bonuses and drafting, Tryon still fell short of what he felt was needed to subdue the regulators. He filled out his ranks with a large number of officer gentlemen. Officers made up a full 10 percent of the Governor's expedition, and the majority of the 1,100 men were from coastal counties.[216] Tryon's greatest advantage as he marched into the backcountry was two brass field pieces and a number of swivel guns. This provided him the standoff combat power required to counter the Regulator's greater numbers.[217]

In April of 1771, Tryon marched his force out of New Bern and into the backcountry. He continued his efforts to bolster his force, holding militia musters in backcountry settlements, although these produced few volunteers. On his way to Hillsborough, Tryon received word that a number of prominent backcountry officials had agreed to begin arbitration with the Regulators. The riots in Hillsborough, and subsequent

---

[214]Kars, 193.

[215]Ibid., 198.

[216]Ibid., 197-198.

[217]Ibid., 193.

unrest in the backcountry, had frightened many officials into making concessions, if only to secure their safety. Tryon was angered by the willingness of these officials to arbitrate, calling the process "unconstitutional, Dishonorable to Government and introductive of a practice the most dangerous to the peace and Happiness of Society."[218] Strangely, Tryon seemed intent to use the army he had assembled; he was looking for a fight.

On 11 May, his forces reached Hillsborough and received word that that a large Regulator force numbering 2,000-3,000 men had surrounded an advanced element of his army near Salisbury. This advanced unit, commanded by General Hugh Waddell, put up no resistance and essentially melted away. A number of Waddell's men joined the Regulators and others simply deserted, returning to their homes.[219]

Upon receiving word of the siege of Waddell's force, Tryon marched his army out of Hillsborough and west towards Salisbury. On the night of 13 May, he camped his force south of the Alamance Creek, just south of present-day Lake Mackintosh. The next morning his force awoke to see a much larger camp of Regulators keeping watch over them nearby.[220] The group of Regulators, roughly 2,000 strong, was hardly a field army. There was no command structure beyond the company level, and when asked to take command, Regulator chief James Hunter replied, "We are all free men; and every one must command himself." This was hardly the statement of an experienced field commander, but the sentiment was one that was deeply held in many frontier Scots-Irish

---

[218] Kars, 196.

[219] William Samuel Powell, *Dictionary of North Carolina Biography Vol. 6* (Chapel Hill: University of North Carolina, 1996), 105.

[220] Kars, 199.

settlements. Most backcountry militia formations were typically ranger companies, the most informal of infantry units.[221] Additionally, Hunter may have not anticipated that a large-scale action was imminent. The experience of the 1768 riot in Hillsborough, and the more recent siege of Waddell's force, likely led Hunter to believe that Tryon's forces would withdraw in the face of superior numbers. Whether they expected a fight or not, the Regulators were ill prepared for one. Most of the men carried "only as many balls in their pouches as they were accustomed to carry with them on a day's hunting."[222]

Over the next two days, the two forces engaged in a staring contest, each assuming the other would back away or disperse. Neither side showed signs of submission, so on 15 May the Regulators sent a petition to Governor Tryon asking that he "lend a kind Ear to the just Complaints of the People."[223] Tryon returned the petition with the message that he would answer their petition the next day. Late the next morning, his answer seemed to come in the form of action rather than words. The governor marched his force in battle formation to within 300 feet of the Regulator camp.[224]

Confused and concerned, the Regulators sent three men to the Governor in hopes of understanding the meaning of his maneuvering. One of the three, a Presbyterian minister named David Caldwell, was returned to the Regulator camp with the answer to

---

[221] Rangers in the eighteenth-century were not the elite regulated infantry they are today. They were instead poorly regulated groups who traveled, or ranged, vast territories serving as scouts and more often, performing the same function as small Indian war parties. They fought in the "Indian style," firing from cover.

[222] Ibid., 201.

[223] Ibid., 199.

[224] Ibid.

the Regulators' petition, while the other two men were held prisoner. Tryon demanded that the Regulators abandon their arms, and surrender their leading men, or face an attack as violators of the recently passed Johnston Riot Act. Stalling, the Regulators sent Caldwell back with a request to exchange prisoners. The Regulators would surrender several officers captured from Waddell's force in exchange for several Regulators held captive by Tryon's men. Although he initially agreed, Tryon seemingly grew impatient since the exchange did not occur immediately. He sent his adjutant to the Regulator camp to inform them that their time was up, and they were to release their prisoners immediately or be fired upon. The Regulator response to Tryon's threat likely sealed their fate. The message the adjutant brought back to Tryon was "fire and be damned."[225] In a fit of anger, Tryon ordered Robert Thompson, one of the men who originally accompanied Caldwell, to be shot. Thompson was escorted to the front of the formation, within view of the Regulator camp, and executed.[226]

Thompson's body still lying on the field, Tryon next sent a sheriff to officially read the Johnston Riot Act to the Regulators, offering one hour to disperse. One hour was not needed. Most accounts of the ensuing battle indicate that sporadic shooting started almost immediately after the reading of the riot act. Accounts of the battle vary widely on most everything else that occurred in the next two hours. One difficulty in obtaining a coherent understanding of the battle is the fact that with no centralized leadership, each Regulator Company acted on the will of its own commander. This provided an individual Regulator in one company with a vastly different experience from a fellow Regulator in

---

[225]Troxler, 109.

[226]Kars, 201.

another company. Another problem is that the only coherent history from the militia's perspective, written by Francois-Xavier Martin in the 1820s, was based almost exclusively on accounts from officers.[227]

All accounts generally agree that the Regulators fought in the "Indian style," hiding behind cover taking pot shots as targets presented themselves. Initially, Tryon's force presented a timid defense. His left wing, under the command of Colonel Edmund Fanning, gave ground, allowing a small group of Regulators to briefly seize control of a small artillery piece. Possession of the artillery piece proved fruitless however, as Fanning's men had the presence of mind to withdraw with the ammunition.[228] Initially, Tryon had difficulty bringing his artillery into action. His guns were slow to commence firing and once they started, their fire was inaccurate and intermittent. This was perhaps because of a general order issued the day before that the firing of five cannon shots would signal the start of the battle.[229] The inexperienced artillery crew evidently felt compelled to obey the order even though the "heavy and dreadful firing"[230] from the Regulators would imply that the battle had started regardless. The battle continued for about two hours before Tryon ordered that the woods be set on fire to flush the Regulators from their cover. As the brush became consumed in flame, the Regulators, most of whom were low on ammunition, began to run.

---

[227] Troxler 109-111.

[228] William Fitch, *Some Neglected History of North Carolina; Being an Account of the Revolution of the Regulators and of the Battle of Alamance, the First Battle of the American Revolution* (New York: Neale Pub. Co., 1905), 222.

[229] Troxler, 111.

[230] Ibid.

Rather than pursue the fleeing Regulators, Tryon halted his force to bury the dead and deal with what prisoners they managed to capture. The number of dead was few, with most accounts holding the number killed on both sides to less than 20. The number of men wounded may have been much larger, perhaps upward of 300.[231] Governor Tryon's first action in regards to prisoners was to hang James Few.[232] While Tryon claimed that the hanging was in response to his troops' desire for vengeance, this seems unlikely. According to Martin's history of the battle, Tryon had to coax and threaten his militia to open fire on the Regulators, at one point shouting, "fire, fire on them or on me."[233] Six additional Regulator prisoners were hung a month later after a summary trial in Hillsborough.

In the weeks that followed what became known as the Battle of Alamance, Tryon's force continued to march through the backcountry, rooting out pockets of resistance, burning the homes and fields of suspected Regulator leaders, and administering loyalty oaths. Tryon's force returned to Hillsborough in July 1771; shortly thereafter, Tryon received word of his impending reassignment as governor of New York. The governor bid his troops a grateful farewell as they paraded through Hillsborough, instructing his second in command to return the force to New Bern. While sporadic resistance movements within the backcountry continued to use the Regulator name,

---

[231]Ibid., 113; Kars, 201.

[232]Kars, 201.

[233]Troxler, 109.

organized resistance of the kind seen in the years leading up to the Battle of Alamance was never seen again.[234] The War of Regulation in North Carolina was over.

Motivating the Regulation

Understanding the motivation of the North Carolina Regulation is difficult. Of the three vigilante movements discussed, the North Carolina Regulation was by far the longest and culminated in the largest outbreak of violence. Additional problems arise when faced with the fact that the Regulators were not a unified or static organization. Loyalties shifted during the regulation. Thomas Polk, credited with being the leader of the earliest manifestation of Regulator activity, later changed sides and supported Governor Tryon's suppression of the movement.[235] While it is important to understand the various motivations for the movement, the focus of this work is to determine ideological links with the American Revolution.

An understanding of the most tangible motivations that led so many backcountry farmers into open rebellion can be gained from three main sources. Between 1766 and 1768, the Regulators published 11 pamphlets, known as Regulator Advertisements in which they communicated their intent to correct perceived oppressions in the backcountry. Although each document is brief, they clearly describe the feelings of backcountry farmers. The second source useful in understanding Regulator motivations is Husband's *An Impartial Relation of the First and Causes of the Recent Differences in Public Affairs Etc.* While his *Impartial Relation* is well organized and thorough in its

---

[234]Kars, 210-211.

[235]Ibid., 126.

communication of backcountry problems, the document should be viewed through the lens of its purpose. The document, written in late 1768, is clearly the commencement of Husband's political campaign to win election to the Lower House of the North Carolina Assembly in June of the next year.[236] That said, Husband's recommendations for resolving the crisis may be viewed as hostage to his ambitions, but his explanation of the problems facing backcountry farmers is consistent with the Regulator Advertisements. The third document, and perhaps the clearest description of Regulator concerns, is the *Instructions from the Subscribers, Inhabitants of Orange County to their Representatives in Assembly;* the marching orders given to Husband and another Regulator representative elected in the summer of 1769.[237]

The three sources are surprisingly consistent in their understanding of backcountry problems, indicating that a few key leaders may have been involved in drafting all three. The backcountry problems as described in the three sources can be distilled into three primary political concerns. Higher than usual taxes were exacted from backcountry farmers without an account being made as to the use of those taxes; debts due to taxes, quitrents, or illegal fees usually resulted in the loss of the debtors' land; and voter intimidation led to the continued election of corrupt officials.[238]

The majority of Regulator communications large and small mention concerns with ever rising taxation. The fifth Regulator Advertisement, written in March 1768 after

---

[236]Troxler, 59-61.

[237]Ibid., 78.

[238]Ibid., 79-80.

Edmund Fanning refused to meet with the Regulators, provides the clearest understanding as to the Regulators' stance on taxation.

> James Watson was sent to Maddock Mills and said that Edmund Fanning looked upon it that the country called him by authority or like as if they had a right to call them to an Accompt.(sic) Not allowing the country the right that they have been entitled to as English subjects, for the King requires no money from His subjects but what they are made sensible what use it's for; we are obliged to seek redress by denying paying any more until we have a full settlement for what is past and have a true regulation with our Officers as our grievances are too many to notify in a small piece of writing.[239]

The reasons for the unusually high taxation also likely vexed the backcountry farmers. Although taxes were raised across the colony to remove an inflated proclamation currency from circulation, the prime driver of higher taxes in the years leading up to the Battle of Alamance was the need to pay for a new mansion for Governor Tryon.[240] Local officials routinely refused to provide backcountry inhabitants with an account of tax money collected. This refusal was an effort to obfuscate corruption, but the established social order also supported this practice. In the minds of the local officials and eastern elite, the demand to account upset the well-established social order so important to eighteenth-century civil society. Fanning, among others, defended the elite's close control of government account books, claiming that the uneducated mind was incapable of understanding their complexities.[241]

---

[239]"22 March 1768, Regulators' Advertisement No. 5 - Address from inhabitants near Haw River to the Orange County Vestry and General Assembly representatives," Colonial North Carolina Records, http://docsouth.unc.edu/csr/index.html/document/csr07-0264 (accessed 16 March 2014).

[240]Kars, 137-138.

[241]Ibid., 136.

Along with rising taxes, almost every communication of Regulator concerns involved illegal fee taking by local officials, a practice that seemingly predated the separation of the Carolinas. While the Regulators hoped to end this practice entirely, the immediate concern was the fact that debts incurred by these illegal fees could result in the loss of their land. This concern is addressed at length in the *Instructions* from Orange County inhabitants. Although the practice of distraint[242] was a source of discontent among the Regulators, they preferred it to the practice of seizing land. To work to replace a cow or a wagon was something entirely different from working to replace a farm, improved by decades of work.[243]

With rising tax rates and a troubling insecurity of property causing such consternation among the backcountry farmers, it was inevitable that their concerns would eventually focus on representation, and more specifically, voting. While Husband's *Impartial Relation* clearly identifies corrupt representatives as a key problem in resolving backcountry issues, he misplaces the blame, likely since his goal was to have himself elected the next year.

> Many are accusing the Legislative Body as the Source of all those woeful Calamities. . . . These, it must be confessed, are the instrumental Cause; they can, yea do impose some of these heavy Burdens. . . . But whence received they- this Power? Is not their Power delegated from the Populace? The original principal Cause is our own blind stupid Conduct.[244]

---

[242]Distraint was the practice of essentially 'pawning' chattels or other moveable goods to the local government in lieu of paying a tax or fee. If unable to pay in specie or note before a designated time, the goods would be auctioned for payment.

[243]Troxler, 80.

[244]"*To the INHABITANTS of the Province of North-Carolina*," Digital-History; North Carolina Regulators, http://www.digitalhistory.uh.edu/disp_textbook.cfm?smtID=3&psid=3878 (accessed 4 April 2014).

In the *Instructions* the inhabitants of Orange County place the blame elsewhere. Since the county sheriff held elections, and votes were cast vocally in public court, they understood it was impossible to elect anyone but persons whom the local officials desired. Casting a vote for a fellow farmer rather than an elite lawyer might result in the voter being subjected to any number of abuses.[245] The farmers of Orange County demanded that their representatives propose legislation changing this mode of election in favor of one in which votes were cast "by tickets."[246]

Even this focus on reforming the election process, while valuable in improving some backcountry conditions, would likely have proven fruitless for the larger concerns. North Carolina in the 1760s had among the least representative governments of all the American colonies. Since the splitting of the Carolinas, North Carolina's leaders pursued a policy of retaining overwhelming political power in the coastal counties. Each time a new backcountry county was established, an eastern county was split in order to maintain electoral dominance within the lower house of the assembly.[247] The truly dire situation of backcountry representation is made clear in an analysis of the 1766 election of lower house representatives. The taxable population of the eastern counties of the colony was a little over 25,000, while the backcountry taxable population was almost equal at roughly 23,500. Eastern counties elected 56 representatives in 1766, while backcountry counties were permitted to elect only 25. Counties like Currituck in the northeast of the colony had 1 representative for every 175 taxable males, while counties like Orange had only 1

---

[245]Troxler, 13.

[246]Ibid., 80.

[247]Ibid., 13.

representative for about every 2,000.[248] With such stark differences in representation, even if Tryon had not dissolved the 1769 assembly, it is doubtful that the few Regulator representatives could have accomplished much.

Of the three vigilante movements discussed, the proximate causes of the North Carolina Regulation bear the most obvious links with the American Revolution. Foremost of these causes was the issue of representation, and where the benefits of elective representation would fall. In Great Britain, the concept of elective representation evolved over time from a medieval concept of representatives benefiting the local populations to the more modern understanding that Parliament represented the nation as a whole, and therefore that the primary duty of representatives was not to their local electorate but to the nation.[249] American representative bodies, on the other hand, moved in the opposite direction, closer to their medieval counterparts. Since most of America was relatively isolated, and since the economic objectives of communities varied more than they did in Great Britain, representatives were expected to pursue the benefit of their electorate and focus less on the good of the entire colony.[250] This fundamental difference about the nature of proper representation likely caused the animosities over both theoretical issues like 'virtual representation' and practical tax measures like the Sugar Act and the Stamp Act.

---

[248]"Report by Charles Woodmason concerning religion in North Carolina, including a list of taxables," Colonial North Carolina Records, http://docsouth.unc.edu/csr/index.html/document/csr07-0152 (accessed 5 April 2014); "Minutes of the Lower House of the North Carolina General Assembly," Colonial North Carolina Records, http://docsouth.unc.edu/csr/index.html/document/csr07-0156. (accessed 5 April 2014).

[249]Bailyn, 162-164.

[250]Ibid.

Since the primary grievances of the Regulators were local, the failure of the representative body of North Carolina to resolve these issues proved to be the final factor in pushing the Regulators beyond legal resistance into open rebellion. The problems that the Regulators had with the corrupt local officials also bear a striking resemblance to concerns of the later revolutionaries. John Trenchard and Thomas Gordon's collection of essays, *Cato's Letters,* eagerly read by radical colonials, warns readers to keep their eyes open for corruption.[251] Drawing correlations between the last days of Rome and the contemporary British government, Gordon believed that corruption, as a tool of tyrants, discouraged civic involvement and instead prepared the populace to "bear with greater tameness, the imperial yoke of servitude."[252]

Contemporaries of the North Carolina Regulation could not help but see the similarities between the backcountry farmer's plight and that of all Americans. The Regulators themselves felt that their resistance was very much in the spirit of the growing resentment of the mother government. Although some of the members of the Sons of Liberty of North Carolina eventually worked against them, the Regulators praised the Sons of Liberty for their defiance of what they saw as an oppressive Parliament. In their first advertisement, the soon-to-be Regulators wrote,

> take this as a maxim that while men are men though you should see all those Sons of Liberty (who has just now redeemed us from tyranny) set in Offices and vested

---

[251] M. N. S. Sellers, *American Republicanism: Roman Ideology in the United States Constitution* (New York: New York University Press, 1994), 105.

[252] John Trenchard, Thomas Gordon, and Ronald Hamowy, *Cato's Letters or Essays on Liberty, Civil and Religious, and Other Important Subjects* (Indianapolis, IN: Liberty Fund, 1995), 121-122.

with power they would soon corrupt again and oppress if they were not called upon to give an account of their Stewardship.[253]

Governor Tryon was concerned in 1768 that people would begin to associate the Regulator struggle with that of the Sons of Liberty and other anti-British movements cropping up all over the colonies. As a result of this fear, Tryon significantly altered his policies towards Presbyterians in the backcountry. The Presbyterian Scots-Irish were particularly supportive of the Sons of Liberty, and the Baptist dominated Regulators were beginning to be seen in the same light, so Tryon convinced the assembly to repeal some of the Vestry laws that prevented Presbyterian ministers from conducting legal marriages.[254] It was through this divide-and-conquer strategy that some of the original leaders of the Regulator movement came to oppose their former followers later. In the stratified loyalties of the clan-like Scots-Irish, loyalty to your religion came first.

Comparisons between the Regulators and the Revolutionaries came from far beyond North Carolina. Outsiders also saw the connection between the two groups. Boston newspapers published pro-Regulator articles,[255] and The London Public Advertiser, in its 13 January 1770 edition, brought news to readers of "Regulators and Assertors of Liberty" in North Carolina. Connecticut scholar Ezra Stiles sympathized with the Regulators. In a diary entry, he observed:

---

[253] August 1766, *Regulators' Advertisement No. 1 – Public notice concerning acts by public officials*. Documenting the American South. University Library, The University of North Carolina at Chapel Hill, http://docsouth.unc.edu/csr/index.html/document/csr07-0129 (accessed 5 April 2014).

[254] Kars, 155-157

[255] Ibid., 209.

> What shall an injured and oppressed people do, when their Petitions Remonstrances and Supplications are unheard and rejected, they insulted by the Crown officers, and Oppression and Tyranny (under the name of Government) continued with Rigour and Egyptian Austerity![256]

The defeat of the Regulators at Alamance seemed only to increase sympathy for the movement, although many could not reconcile the open violence of the Regulators with ideals of liberty and freedom from oppression. In the minds of men like James Iredell, suppression of the Regulation was a necessity in favor of law and order.[257] The future Supreme Court Justice was not yet ready for rebellion in 1771. The local nature of the Regulator grievances, along with the antagonisms of an overly aggressive colonial Governor, drove the North Carolina Regulators to make the transition from peaceful remonstrance to resistance and ultimately violence in a period of only a decade. Their open violence against colonial forces was inexcusable to many who would themselves, only a short time later, choose the same option. It was perhaps the distance between the colonies and England, as well as the difficulties of organizing a resistance among the thirteen colonies, that delayed the violence of Lexington and Concord for four more years.

---

[256]Ibid., 208.

[257]Ibid.

CHAPTER 7

THE VIGILANTES GO TO WAR

For the Scots-Irish of the colonial backcountry, their resort to violence in the 1760s did not so much mark the end of something as it did the beginning. Four short years after the defeat of the North Carolina Regulators at Alamance, a group of Massachusetts colonists made a very similar stand against British Regulars at Lexington and Concord. A little more than a year after that, the American colonies declared independence from Britain and thus sparked a seven-year war that eventually involved fighting in almost every corner of the colonies. The former vigilantes of the backcountry were not immune from the fighting and quickly confronted the reality of having to choose sides. Choosing sides was a very real possibility, far from the simplistic depiction of American colonists against the British Army; the War for Independence saw considerable fighting between American colonists as well. It did not take long for the former vigilantes to find themselves very much a part of the conflict. As early as August of 1775, former Regulator James Mayson reported to Major Andrew Williamson that he was tracking a Loyalist "Body of Men" headed towards Augusta.[258]

After having spent a fair amount of time in gaining an understanding of the vigilantes and their motivations, it seems only natural to be curious as to where they ended up during the Revolution. The task of tracking down almost 1,000 individuals proved to be insurmountable within the scope of this thesis; however, it was possible to

---

[258] "Williamson, Andrew, orders to John Caldwell, Advising him that a body of loyalists are marching on Augusta," Robert W. Gibbes Collection of Revolutionary War Manuscripts, http://www.archivesindex.sc.gov/onlinearchives/Thumbnails.aspx?recordId=174955 (accessed 22 April 2014).

find evidence of a large number of these vigilantes during the war. The number, while still short of being a representative sample is large enough to be of value in gaining a better insight of how their 1760s ideologies played out in the 1770s and beyond.

The Paxton "Patriots"

As discussed before, the identities of very few Paxton Boys is known for certain. The Paxton Militia Regimental commander, Rev. John Elder, while likely not involved in the massacre, may have been involved in the march on Philadelphia. Elder's Company commanders, Lazarus Stewart, Matthew Smith, and Asher Clayton were more likely involved in both events. Beyond these men, the only other certain name associated with the insurrection is James Gibson, who along with Stewart wrote the *Declaration* and *Remonstrance*.[259] Born about 1706, Elder was far too old to serve the Patriot cause in the field. Instead, he held a Colonel's commission, was the Chairman of the Committee of Public Safety for the Paxton area, and recruited actively among his congregation. He died in 1792 and thus, little else is known of his wartime service.[260]

As the Continental Army slowly came into existence in the aftermath of Lexington and Concord, Smith found himself commanding one of two companies raised from Lancaster County. Once the Pennsylvania Regiment assembled, they marched to Boston to assist in the siege of the city. Smiths' company was pulled away from siege duty in September in order to join Colonel Benedict Arnold's force on their invasion of

---

[259]Kenney, 143-144.

[260]Cavaioli, 81-82.

Canada. Through the course of his service, Smith rose from Captain to Lieutenant Colonel of the 9th Pennsylvania Regiment, eventually resigning in February of 1778.[261]

Stewart's loyalties are difficult to understand, if he had any. After the Paxton insurrection, Stewart fled north into the Wyoming valley and became an outlaw, accused of countless acts of violence. In the summer of 1778, a number of British Loyalists and Indians from New York attacked settlers in the Wyoming valley, and on 3 July, Stewart died at their hands.[262] That Stewart died fighting against the Loyalists is likely beyond debate; however, fighting Loyalists does not make him a Patriot. There is no record of Stewart serving the Patriot cause before, even though there were opportunities. A year prior to his death, the Wyoming militia was called to join Washington's forces, but Stewart remained in the valley. Based on his involvement in the massacre of the Conestoga, numerous instances of violence in the backcountry, and his ultimate death, it is easy to imagine Stewart as a man without a cause, always in search of a fight.

Little at all is known of Asher Clayton before, during, or after the Revolution. He was a militia company commander under Elder, but perhaps served as a militia colonel at times during the French and Indian War.[263] While there is an Asher Clayton of New Jersey who served in the New Jersey line during the War for Independence, this is likely

---

[261] Ibid., 85-87; Fold3, "Matthew Smith," Compiled Service Records of Soldiers Who Served in the American Army During the Revolutionary War, http://www.fold3.com/image/21340031/ (accessed 20 April 2014).

[262] Ibid., 87-90.

[263] William Stone, *Life of Joseph Brant-Thayendanegea* (St. Clair Shores, MI: Scholarly Press, 1970), 327.

a different man as tax records and census substitutes record both men living in different states at the same time.[264]

Of the known Paxton Boys, little can be assumed about the whole. An elderly recruiter, an early quitting officer, a violent maniac, and a ghost can tell us little of the men who marched on Philadelphia in 1764. In an effort to gain a better understanding of the loyalties of the backcountry Scots-Irish around Paxton, the investigation was centered on people who attended the Paxton Presbyterian Church, led by Elder. While it could be assumed that a number of these men were involved in the insurrection, it is unlikely that they all were. In an effort to avoid wrongfully accusing the dead, the names of the men used in establishing a sample will not be used, only numbers will be referenced.

Roughly 700 people are buried in the cemetery, which sits adjacent to the same church building used by Elder and his parishioners. Of the roughly 700 internments, 56 are for males whose birth and death dates would have permitted participation in both the insurrection and the Revolution.[265] Thirty-one of these can be confirmed to have served the Patriot cause. The number of Patriots among these men might well be higher; however, the sources used make it difficult to identify men who died before the first congressionally authorized pensions in the late 1820s. The men who served militarily

---

[264] "1781 Schedule" Pennsylvania, Northumberland County, Tax and Exoneration, 1768-1801, http://search.ancestry.com/search/db.aspx?dbid=2497&enc=1 (accessed 20 April 2014); "1781 Tax List" New Jersey, Monmouth County, Census Substitutes Index, 1643-1890, http://search.ancestry.com/search/db.aspx?dbid=3562&enc=1 (accessed 20 April 2014).

[265] "Paxton Presbyterian Church," Find-A-Grave - All Internments, http://www.findagrave.com/cgi-bin/fg.cgi?page=gsr&GScid=2240320 (accessed 20 April 2014).

overwhelmingly served in the Pennsylvania Flying Camps.[266] A number of these men were wounded during the course of their service, and despite early setbacks and frustrations with how they were being used, most of these men from Paxton remained in the service until at least 1778.[267]

Admittedly, sources covering Pennsylvania Loyalists are few, yet the mere fact that the investigation was based on men who were buried in Paxton means it is unlikely that any of them were Loyalists. Further study into records of migrations from Pennsylvania to Canada or back to England could uncover possible Loyalists from among the Paxton men. The impression gained from examining the records of these men buried in Paxton is that they were largely Patriots and served honorably. Impressions gained from the accounts of contemporaries also tell the story of overwhelming Scots-Irish patriotism. In 1778 a Hessian soldier serving the British army wrote that the war was "nothing more or less than a Scotch Irish Presbyterian rebellion."[268]

---

[266] A flying camp was a perpetually mobile force of cavalry and dragoon reserves. The name came from the fact that since they were always mobile, even in winter, they never set up camps like infantry forces did. The early flying camps established by Washington never really achieved their purpose and essentially disbanded; David Fischer, *Washington's Crossing* (New York: Oxford University Press, 2004), 85, 275.

[267] "Assorted Names," Compiled Service Records of Soldiers Who Served in the American Army During the Revolutionary War, http://www.fold3.com/title_470/revolutionary_war_service_records/ (accessed 14 April 2014); "Assorted Names," Revolutionary War Pension and Bounty-Land Warrant Application Files, http://www.fold3.com/title_467/revolutionary_war_pensions/ (accessed 14 April 2014).

[268] David Wilson, *United Irishmen, United States: Immigrant Radicals in the Early Republic* (Dublin: Four Courts Press, 1998), 14.

Civil War Among the Regulators

As the British commenced the main effort of their southern campaign in 1780, it was with the understanding that General Sir Henry Clinton's forces would be significantly augmented with Loyalist militias from the Carolinas.[269] In May, as American Major General Benjamin Lincoln surrendered Charleston, Clinton tasked Major Patrick Ferguson with recruiting Loyalist forces in the South Carolina backcountry in preparation for an invasion of North Carolina.[270] Ferguson likely had little understanding of the dynamics of the backcountry, or that its inhabitants had already fought and brokered a tentative peace. As he rode into the dense piney forests of the back settlements, he stoked the embers of anger that remained from the early fighting in 1775.

The war in the south started with a Regulator. In June 1775, Major James Mayson, who lived near the village of Ninety-Six received orders from the council of safety to seize Fort Charlotte just to the south along the Savannah river. The fort contained only a token garrison, but housed considerable stores of powder and ammunition, as well as several artillery pieces. Mayson, along with fellow Regulator Moses Kirkland, easily took Fort Charlotte without any fighting. They left a small garrison at Fort Charlotte to retain it, and returned to the fort at Ninety-Six with large quantities of powder and ammunition. Once they arrived at Fort Ninety-Six, Kirkland apparently had a change of heart and gathered a Loyalist force from along the northern side of the Saluda and captured the fort and Mayson. There was no bloodshed, and

---

[269] John Ferling, *Almost a Miracle* (New York: Oxford University Press, 2007), 126-127.

[270] Ruma Chopra, *Unnatural Rebellion: Loyalists in New York City During the Revolution* (Charlottesville: University of Virginia Press, 2011), 190.

Mayson was released a few days later.[271] The two would confront each other again a few short months later. In November, Patrick Cunningham, brother of Robert Cunningham the Regulator, gathered a force of Loyalists and seized several supply wagons headed from Fort Charlotte to the Cherokee territory. The shipment was intended to help broker neutrality with the Cherokee but it never got there. Mayson again raised several hundred men at Ninety-Six, where Cunningham surprised him before he could ready his force to march. The two sides exchanged gunfire for the better part of two days before the belligerents agreed to a truce. The casualty toll for both sides was relatively low, five men killed and perhaps 30 wounded.[272] Few men from the surrounding area were involved in the fighting on either side.[273]

With both Patriots and Loyalists departing Fort Ninety-Six in the wake of the truce, Richard Richardson, the Regulator sympathizer who negotiated the truce between the Regulators and Moderators, raised 2,500 men to run the Loyalists out of the area. The Snow Campaign, as it became known was unsuccessful in subduing Cunningham and his fellow chiefs, but was successful in dampening zeal of the Loyalists. Most Loyalists simply decided to return to their home lives and watch how things developed, while others, including Cunningham took refuge in Cherokee territory.[274]

---

[271]Gordon, 22-24.

[272]Ibid., 29-30.

[273]Walter Edgar, *Partisans and Redcoats: The Southern Conflict that Turned the Tide of the American Revolution* (New York: Harper Collins, 2001), 32.

[274]Ibid., 33.

There were only a few engagements in the South Carolina backcountry between the end of the Snow Campaign and the fall of Charleston in May of 1780. The backcountry was largely under control of the Patriots who were mostly concerned with protecting the coast, and mitigating the threat of the Cherokee to their west. Once Charleston fell, however, Loyalists in the backcountry, who had been content to bide their time, broke loose. The backcountry exploded in partisan violence. By the time American Major General Nathanael Greene arrived in the southern backcountry, things had become so bad that he wrote,

> The Whigs and Tories pursue one another with the most relentless fury, killing and destroying each other whenever they meet. Indeed a great part of this country is already laid waste and in the utmost danger of becoming a desert. The great bodies of militia that have been in service this year. . . have laid waste the country.[275]

The strategic missteps of Major Ferguson and British Lieutenant Colonel Banastre Tarleton in failing to understand the complexities of the southern backcountry likely helped tip the scales of partisans to the Patriot cause. The shocking death toll dealt by Tarleton at the Battle of Waxhaws, and Ferguson's threat of invasion of the Watauga settlement are generally credited with considerable influence in the turning the backcountry against the British.[276]

Despite the general turn towards Patriot sympathies, conditions within the backcountry remained contentious until the end of British occupation in December

---

[275]Noam Chomsky and Edward S. Herman, *After the Cataclysm, Postwar Indochina and the Construction of Imperial Ideology* (Montreal: Black Rose Books, 1979), 43.

[276]Bruce Lancaster and J. H. Plumb, *The American Revolution* (Boston: Houghton Mifflin Co., 2001), 289; Scoggins, 46.

1782.[277] Some have even described the backcountry partisan conflict on 1780-82 as a civil war. Despite the split nature of loyalties within backcountry South Carolina, former Regulators were overwhelmingly Patriots.[278] Conversely, the Moderators who stood against the Regulators during the 1760s were predominantly Loyalists.[279] According to Richard Maxwell Brown, of the 118 Regulators, 69 were Patriots and 6 were Loyalist.[280] Unfortunately, Brown does not include an explanation of his method for determining the loyalties of the Regulators.

In reviewing pension and land grant applications, available service record information, and Robert Lambert's work on South Carolina Loyalists, Brown's conclusion is confirmed albeit the numbers differ slightly. Of the Regulators that can be reliably identified by name and location, forty-one were determined to have served the Patriot cause either militarily or politically. Nine were determined to have either serviced Loyalist forces, or returned to England.[281]

In understanding these loyalties, it is important to note that loyalties seemed to run along family lines. The Cunningham family was entirely Loyalist. Robert

---

[277]Edgar, 137.

[278]Brown, 123.

[279]Edgar, 123.

[280]Brown, 123.

[281]"Assorted Names," Compiled Service Records of Soldiers Who Served in the American Army During the Revolutionary War, http://www.fold3.com/title_470/revolutionary_war_service_records/ (accessed 14 April 2014); "Assorted Names," Revolutionary War Pension and Bounty-Land Warrant Application Files, http://www.fold3.com/title_467/revolutionary_war_pensions/ (accessed 14 April 2014); Brown, *Passim*; Lambert, *Passim*.

Cunningham eventually attained the rank of Brigadier General of militia. Conversely the McGraw family were entirely Patriots, sending Edward, Enoch, and William to field service in the South Carolina line as well as the militia. While Moses Kirkland turned against the Patriot cause early, his relatives Joseph and William both served as Captains in the Patriot militia.[282] Moses' departure from the family line can largely be explained by his never-ending pursuit of his own self-interests. Once captured by the Patriots, he offered to switch back to their camp but was turned down. His original switch to the Loyalist side has been described as a response to Mayson receiving a higher commission than him at the outset of the war.[283]

Most of the former Regulators served in local militias for three to six months terms of service. One of these militiamen, Enoch Andrews served under Brigadier General Francis Marion's command for some time.[284] Some, on the other hand, served more conspicuously in the South Carolina line regiments. Two of the former Regulators, Thomas Woodward and John Owens were killed in action in 1779 and 1781 respectively.[285] Far from being only interested in a good fight however, the Regulators continued to serve the new Republic off the battlefield. Twelve Regulators served on the 1st and 2nd Provincial Congresses.[286]

---

[282]Ibid.

[283]Brown, 129.

[284]"Enoch Andrews," Compiled Service Records of Soldiers Who Served in the American Army During the Revolutionary War, http://www.fold3.com/image/23621281/ (accessed 4 November 2013).

[285]Brown, 131.

[286]Ibid., 124.

Although loyalties seemingly ran along family lines, the sheer number of Regulators who sided with the Patriot cause, as well as the corresponding loyalties of their former foes, the Moderators, tends to indicate that the Regulators supported the Patriot cause for reasons beyond family ties. Furthermore, their willingness to serve for, and alongside with low country elites who had previously ignored their concerns shows that they could temporarily put aside quarrels in order to pursue their larger ideology.

Exodus to Patriotism

Unlike the Paxton Boys or South Carolina Regulators, the North Carolina Regulators were not a shy group of men. Culling through the signatures of the Regulator Advertisements, letters from Governor William Tryon, pardons, and other such sources yields 846 names associated with the movement. It is important to note however, that simply because one signed his name to a Regulator Advertisement, does not mean that he was present at the Battle of Alamance. It is likely that if one were to converse with all 846 men, several would be surprised that many historians call them Regulators. Regardless, the men all seem to have indicated a more than passing support of the Regulator causes, and as such tracking their revolutionary activities can still provide a useful glimpse into the Regulators post-Alamance. Eight hundred forty-six names proved entirely too many to attempt a reliable identification, so a selection of ninety names was taken for closer study. Of these 90 men, only 29 were positively identified by name and location. A likely explanation for the low identification rate is that after the defeat at

Alamance, and Tryon's campaign of persecution afterwards, many Regulators left North Carolina for Georgia, South Carolina, and what is today Tennessee.[287]

Of the 29 men who could be identified, all of them were Patriots.[288] It must be assumed that some of those 61 men who could not be identified were Loyalists, but sources identifying Loyalist militia members are few, while sources identifying Patriot militia members are many. Even with this assumption, it is unlikely that many served the Loyalist cause. Governor Tryon's replacement, Joseph Martin assumed that the Regulators would flock to the King's defense. In February 1776 he sent out a call for the Regulators to assemble with the Highland Scots of Cross Creek. Of the 3,000 Regulators Martin expected to show, fewer than 200 arrived.[289] Although the record is not entirely clear, Regulator leader James Hunter may have been among those who arrived in Cross Creek.[290] The loyalties of Hunter are hotly debated. Not just because of a lack of hard evidence, but because the hard evidence that remains paints a somewhat confusing picture. Although Hunter may have been among those captured near Cross Creek in

---

[287]Kars, 211.

[288]"Assorted Names," Compiled Service Records of Soldiers Who Served in the American Army During the Revolutionary War, http://www.fold3.com/title_470/revolutionary_war_service_records/ (accessed 14 April 2014); "Assorted Names," Revolutionary War Pension and Bounty-Land Warrant Application Files, http://www.fold3.com/title_467/revolutionary_war_pensions/ (accessed 14 April 2014).

[289]Duane Gilbert Meyer, *The Highland Scots of North Carolina, 1732-1776* (Chapel Hill: University of North Carolina Press, 1961), 156.

[290]Marshall De Lancey Haywood, *Governor William Tryon, and His Administration in the Province of North Carolina, 1765-1771. Services in a Civil Capacity and Military Career As Commander-in-Chief of Colonial Forces Which Suppressed the Insurrection of the Regulators* (Raleigh: E. M. Uzzell, 1903), 173.

1776, he later took an oath to the state and ultimately served Guilford County as Sheriff.[291]

Herman Husband, the ideological inspiration of the Regulators fled Alamance just prior to the battle. He likely understood that to remain in North Carolina meant certain imprisonment or death, and he moved to Pennsylvania. He took up the Patriot cause quickly, supporting the radicals within the colony. In 1778 he managed to get elected to the Pennsylvania assembly where he remained a staunch Whig throughout the conflict. Husband never could shake his rebellious ways and he quickly became involved in the Whiskey Rebellion. He spent time in jail for his participation and died days after his release in 1795.[292]

Other Regulators lived more upstanding lives. After the execution of his brother, James, immediately following the Battle of Alamance, William Few fled with another brother, Benjamin to Georgia. Once the War for Independence commenced William and his brother both received Lieutenant Colonel's commissions with William serving in the prestigious dragoons. William did not limit his contributions to military service. Apparently a gifted politician, he served in the Georgia provincial congress of 1776, in the Continental Congress, and ultimately became one of the first United States Senators from Georgia.[293]

---

[291] Sallie Walker Stockard, *The History of Guilford County, North Carolina* (Knoxville, TN: Gaut-Ogden Co., 1902), 36.

[292] Kars, 212.

[293] Andrew R. Dodge, *Biographical Directory of the United States Congress: 1774-2005; the Continental Congress, Sept. 5, 1774 to Oct. 21, 1788, and the Congress of the United States from the First Through the One Hundred Eighth Congresses, March 4, 1789 to Jan. 3, 2005 Inclusive* (Washington, DC: U.S. G.P.O., 2005), 1048.

Regulator Robert Caruthers perhaps provides the perfect example of the Scots-Irish experience in the backcountry and the early United States. Born in 1750 in Lancaster County, Pennsylvania, his parents moved with him when he was young to Mecklenburg County in southwestern North Carolina. He was one of the "Black Boys of Mecklenburg" and served five tours of duty during the Revolution. He participated in several battles, including Kings Mountain, which marked the death of Ferguson and his Loyalist militia. After the war, he followed the path of the over mountain men, settling in Tennessee, just south of Nashville.[294] According to a Williamson County, Tennessee historical marker, his son served in the War of 1812, and his grandson was a Confederate Civil War veteran.[295]

On the other side of the Regulator conflict, Edmund Fanning, who incurred the wrath of the Regulators of Orange County, was one of the most active Loyalists of the war. Fanning accompanied Governor Tryon to New York after the Battle of Alamance, working as his secretary. He, along with Tryon, received commissions as colonels, and Fanning raised the King's American Regiment of Loyalists.[296] Fanning was not the only Loyalist among Tryon's former force, but there was more than one future Patriot among Tryon's men that day. It is perhaps accurate to say that in 1775, Tryon's former men were just as divided as the Regulators.

---

[294]"Robert Carothers," Revolutionary War Pension and Bounty-Land Warrant Application Files, http://www.fold3.com/image/13011575/ (accessed 10 April 2014).

[295]"Carothers Family Marker," Tennessee Historical Markers, http://www.waymarking.com/waymarks/WMJHAZ_Carothers_Family_Franklin_TN (accessed 20 April 2014).

[296]Chopra, 115.

It is difficult to draw any sort of convincing conclusion based solely on the revolutionary experience of the known North Carolina Regulators. It is reasonable to suggest that some were Loyalists, and a few more were Patriots, but the majority likely sat out the conflict, reluctant to put their lives and fortunes on the line again so recently after their defeat at Alamance. Baptists in the backcountry saw a resurgence of their pacifist traditions in the wake of Alamance,[297] and some Regulators headed to the western frontier establishing the Watauga settlement.[298] In the years after the War for Independence, one man aptly summed up the sense of defeat and frustration that ran deep in the minds of former Regulators, "I have fought for my country, and fought for my king; and have been whipped both times."[299]

Strain of Violence

The North Carolina Regulators were simply too shaken by their defeat at Alamance to respond overwhelmingly for one side or the other during the Revolution, yet the Paxton Boys seemed to have been unanimously in support of the Patriot cause. The South Carolina Regulators stand between these two groups. It seems the preponderance of them fought, and fought as Patriots, but with a few highly notable exceptions. Although the ideologies and motivations that drove their vigilante actions are indelibly linked with those that caused the Revolution, it seems as if the actual war time

---

[297]Troxler, 150-151.

[298]Brenda C. Calloway and Jay Robert Reese, *America's First Western Frontier, East Tennessee: A Story of the Early Settlers and Indians of East Tennessee* (Johnson City, TN: Overmountain Press, 1989), 77.

[299]Kars, 214.

experiences of these vigilantes suggests that violence acts as a valve which releases the pressure of discontent. The 1771 Battle of Alamance took the starch out of the North Carolinian backcountry inhabitants, while the massacre of the Conestoga and march on Philadelphia of 1764 was long enough before the Revolution for the pressure of discontent to build again.

CHAPTER 8

CONCLUSION

The examination of the causes, course, and conclusions of these three Scots-Irish vigilante movements clearly indicate that they were ideologically aligned with some of the more popular understandings of the American Revolution. The belief in representative government, and that all governments were accountable to the people was a central belief in both the Revolution, and the three vigilante movements discussed. The influence of classical Greek philosophers, and more importantly, John Locke is evident in this shared understanding of the role of government.[300] The willingness of the Scots-Irish to resort to violence once peaceful means were exhausted indicates that they were influenced to some degree by the same Whig ideology that drove Jefferson and Adams. While the savage Paxton Boys were quicker to ire than their southern counterparts, even they quickly returned to peaceful resolutions when they sensed genuine negotiation was possible.[301] The Regulators of the Carolinas are perhaps the better example of restraint before rebellion. The North Carolina Regulators in particular systematically tried all peaceful means before finally resorting to open violence, essentially making rebellion the choice of the oppressive government, rather than of the disgruntled people. This duty to attempt peaceful recourse is a fundamental part of the Whig theory of the relationship between the governed and the government.[302]

---

[300]Bailyn, 25-28.

[301]Kenny, 159-163.

[302]Kars, 133-134.

The similar ideologies of the Scots-Irish vigilantes and the Revolutionaries of 1775-76 are also evident in the aspects of their governments that they saw as oppressive. The unifying theme of all of the vigilante movements was a frustration with a lack of effective representation for the backcountry inhabitants, but concerns over inequitable tax burdens, judicial jurisdictions and tenures, and corruption are all motivations seen in both the vigilante movements and the Revolution. It is perhaps because of these obvious similarities that so many contemporaries saw the connections that have been obscured by time.

Understanding that the American Revolution was the result of multiple converging ideologies, it is important to understand where the Scots-Irish vigilantes fit within this revolutionary brotherhood. The zeal with which the South Carolina Regulators participated in colonial elections while also rebelling, and the North Carolina Regulator desire to restore, not overthrow legal government shows that the Carolinian Scots-Irish were perhaps more reluctant revolutionaries, like the New Yorkers who later cautiously walked the road to rebellion.[303] Conversely, the speed with which the Paxton Boys resorted to violence and the apparent unanimity with which they supported the Revolutionary cause indicates that they were radical revolutionaries of the likes of Samuel Adams. Just as the American Revolution cannot be seen as a single ideology leading from oppression to independence, the three vigilante movements discussed, however similar, were separate movements guided by different albeit aligned motivations.

---

[303]Tiedemann, 6-7.

Although it would be beyond the scope of this thesis, a further analysis would likely uncover that the building sense of separateness between the British subjects of the isles and their American cousins, and the separateness between the coastal cultures and the backcountry cultures enabled the dysfunctional relationship that developed. This development of a sense of separateness cannot be blamed only on the side that assumes the role of oppressor. The very name "Scotch-Irish," self-applied by the Ulster Scot immigrants[304] indicates that they were partially responsible for establishing a defiantly separate identity. It is in this sense of separateness that the rifts within the society can grow between two people until such a point as they can no longer be governed under one system.

The vigilantes universally failed to accomplish all of their goals. While the South Carolina Regulators achieved some fairly significant resolutions to some of their grievances, other grievances continued to be issues well into the establishment of the state. The other two vigilante movements accomplished little beyond shocking colonial authorities into operating more carefully. These unresolved problems continued to fester below the surface until in 1775, the same problems and ideologies that gave rise to the vigilante movements exploded on a much larger scale. Although many of the former adversaries of the Scots-Irish cast their lots with the Patriots, the backcountry inhabitants clearly saw that for most of them, their best interests were in supporting the men who only years before had oppressed or neglected them. This is an indication that although the

---

[304] James Leyburn, *The Scotch-Irish: A Social History* (Chapel Hill: University of North Carolina Press, 1962), 327-328. The immigrants took the name Scotch-Irish to clearly indicate that they were not Irish, and not Scottish, as they were commonly called by English settlers.

Scots-Irish had strong clannish tendencies, their loyalties during the American Revolution came more directly from their ideological beliefs than from clannish senses of kinship.

The heavy involvement of Scots-Irishmen in later rebellions like the Whiskey Rebellion, the Watauga Association, and the failed state of Franklin indicate that to some degree they were forever in search of Lockean perfection; a self-governing society with minimal authority over the governed. Their understanding of self-government seemed to be far more local than other revolutionaries at the time. Because they had such a deep seeded clannish culture, self-rule to the Scots-Irish meant rule by, or at least compatible with, Scots-Irish values. James Hunter's famous words at the Battle of Alamance could be seen as indicative of the Scots-Irish concept of government as a whole: "We are all freemen, and everyone must command himself." Their desire to live beyond the control of others is likely what so attracted them to the American backcountry, yet the backcountry only offered them the chance to relive hundreds of years of prejudice and violence in a few short decades.

With the exception of a few isolated groups, Americans have long since lost any ability to legitimately claim one ethnicity or another. While there are plenty who claim to be Scots-Irish, the truth of the matter is that most Americans are descendants of countless ethnic groups. What seems more likely is that by identifying with a particular ethnicity, modern Americans are in fact making an ideological statement rather than a genetic one. Most ethnicities have a long list of stereotypes associated with them, some positive and some negative. To some people, the positive stereotypes of a particular ethnicity speak to them in deep and meaningful ways. By identifying themselves with an ethnicity,

Americans are in a way communicating what they feel is important. For most of the history of the United States, the Census has differentiated only by race, not ethnicity. Somewhat counter intuitively, as questions of race and ethnicity have become less and less important from a legal or civil rights standpoint, the Census has offered more and more ways to respond to both. The 2000 census allowed Americans to identify their ethnicity among a long list. In it, the people of the Appalachians, one of the most isolated regions of the United States, made a unique ideological statement. This region, whose inhabitants could more easily make claims of being legitimately Scots-Irish, overwhelmingly reported that their ethnicity was "American."[305] This is likely a statement indicating approval of those ideals that are associated with the American identity, and with the American Revolution.

    The value of gaining a better understanding of the Scots-Irish vigilantes of the 1760s is the value of understanding ourselves. Although the American identity is inherited from a wide variety of cultures and ethnicities, as well as by our own American experience, the Scots-Irish almost unanimously shared the values that are most closely associated with being American. For good, or bad, these values make us prone to divide, quarrel, resist authority, and at times fight. These values gave rise to countless cases of vigilante violence, secession movements, and a civil war. Yet, the American identity that leads us to focus on philosophical and political differences is the very ideological thread that binds us together.

---

[305] Woodard, 8.

BIBLIOGRAPHY

Books

Alden, John, and Wendell Stephenson. *The South in the Revolution: 1763-1789.* Baton Rouge, LA: Louisiana State University Press, 1976.

Anderson, Fred. *Crucible of War: The Seven Years' War and the Fate of Empire in British North America, 1754-1766.* New York: Alfred A. Knopf, 2000.

———. *The War that Made America: A Short History of the French and Indian War.* New York: Viking, 2005.

Bailyn, Bernard. *The Ideological Origins of the American Revolution.* Cambridge, MA: Belknap Press of Harvard University Press, 1967.

Bassani, Luigi. *Liberty, State and Union: The Political Theory of Thomas Jefferson.* Macon, GA: Mercer University Press, 2010.

Blethen, Tyler, and Curtis Wood. *From Ulster to Carolina: The Migration of the Scotch-Irish to Southwestern North Carolina.* Raleigh: North Carolina Department of Cultural Resources, Division of Archives and History, 1998.

Brown, Richard Maxwell. *The South Carolina Regulators.* Cambridge: Belknap Press of Harvard University Press, 1963.

———. *Strain of Violence Historical Studies of American Violence and Vigilantism.* New York: Oxford University Press, 1975.

Brubaker, John. *Massacre of the Conestogas: On the Trail of the Paxton Boys in Lancaster County.* Charleston, SC: History Press, 2010.

Byrd, William, and William K. Boyd. *William Byrd's Histories of the Dividing Line Betwixt Virginia and North Carolina.* Raleigh, NC: North Carolina Historical Commission, 1929.

Byrne, James, Philip Coleman, and Jason King. *Ireland and the Americas: Culture, Politics, and History: A Multidisciplinary Encyclopedia.* Santa Barbara, CA: ABC-CLIO, 2008.

Calloway, Brenda C., and Jay Robert Reese. *America's First Western Frontier, East Tennessee: A Story of the Early Settlers and Indians of East Tennessee.* Johnson City, TN: Overmountain Press, 1989.

Chomsky, Noam, and Edward S. Herman. *After the Cataclysm, Postwar Indochina and the Construction of Imperial Ideology.* Montreal: Black Rose Books, 1979.

Chopra, Ruma. *Unnatural Rebellion: Loyalists in New York City During the Revolution.* Charlottesville, VA: University of Virginia Press, 2011.

Cramer, Clayton E. *Armed America: The Remarkable Story of How and Why Guns Became As American As Apple Pie.* Nashville, TN: Nelson Current, 2006.

Dunaway, Wayland Fuller. *The Scotch-Irish of Colonial Pennsylvania.* Chapel Hill: University of North Carolina Press, 1944.

Dunbar, John. *The Paxton Papers.* The Hague: Martinus Nijoff, 1957.

Edgar, Walter B. *Partisans and Redcoats: The Southern Conflict That Turned the Tide of the American Revolution.* New York: Morrow, 2001.

Ferling, John. *Almost a Miracle.* New York: Oxford University Press, 2007.

Fitch, William Edward. *Some Neglected History of North Carolina; Being an Account of the Revolution of the Regulators and of the Battle of Alamance, the First Battle of the American Revolution.* New York: Neale, 1905.

Flemming, Thomas. *A Disease in the Public Mind: A New Understanding of Why We Fought the Ciil War.* New York: Da Capo Press, 2013.

Franklin, Benjamin. *A Narrative of the Late Massacres, in Lancaster County, of a Number of Indians, Friends of This Province, by Persons Unknown With Some Observations on the Same.* Philadelphia: Franklin and Hall, 1764.

Frantz, John B., and William Pencak. *Beyond Philadelphia: The American Revolution in the Pennsylvania Hinterland.* University Park, PA: Pennsylvania State University Press, 1998.

González, Justo L. *Story of Christianity: The Early Church to the Present Day.* Peabody, MA: Prince Press, 2010.

Gordon, John W. *South Carolina and the American Revolution: A Battlefield History.* Columbia: University of South Carolina Press, 2003.

Gragg, Rod. *Forged in Faith.* New York: Howard Books, 2010.

Gregg, Alexander. *History of the Old Cheraws.* New York: Richardson and Company, 1867.

Hannah, Wayne, and Maureen Dorcy Hannah. *A Hannah Family of West Virginia.* Shelton, WA: W. and M. Hannah, 2000.

Heywood, Marshall De Lancey. *Governor William Tryon, and His Administration in the Province of North Carolina, 1765-1771. Services in a Civil Capacity and Military*

Career As Commander-in-Chief of Colonial Forces Which Suppressed the Insurrection of the Regulators. Raleigh, NC: E. M. Uzzell, 1903.

Heywood, Samuel, and Capel Lofft. *The Right of Protestant Dissenters to a Compleat Toleration Asserted Containing an Historical Account of the Test Laws, and Shweing the Injustice, Inexpediency, and Folly of the Sacramental Test . . . With an Answer to the Objection from the Act of Union with Scotland.* London: J. Johnson, 1789.

Himes, Andrew. *The Sword of the Lord: The Roots of Fundamentalism in an American Family.* Seattle, WA: Chiara Press, 2011.

Hinderaker, Eric, and Peter C. Mancall. *At the Edge of Empire: The Backcountry in British North America.* Baltimore: Johns Hopkins University Press, 2003.

Isaacson, Walter. *Benjamin Franklin: An American Life.* New York: Simon and Schuster, 2003.

Johnson, George Lloyd. *The Frontier in the Colonial South: South Carolina Backcountry, 1736-1800.* Westport, CT: Greenwood Press, 1997.

Kars, Marjoleine. *Breaking Loose Together The Regulator Rebellion in Pre-Revolutionary North Carolina.* Chapel Hill, NC: University of North Carolina Press, 2002.

Kennedy, David, Lizabeth Cohen, and Thomas Andrew Bailey. *The American Pageant: A History of the American People. Vol. I.* Boston, MA: Wadsworth Cengage Learning, 2010.

Kenny, Kevin. *Peaceable Kingdom Lost: The Paxton Boys and the Destruction of William Penn's Holy Experiment.* Oxford: Oxford University Press, 2009.

Klein, Rachel N. *Unification of a Slave State: The Rise of the Planter Class in the South Carolina Backcountry, 1760-1808.* Chapel Hill: University of North Carolina Press, 1990.

Krawczynski, Keith. *William Henry Drayton: South Carolina Revolutionary Patriot.* Baton Rouge, LA: Louisiana State University Press, 2001.

Kumamoto, Robert. *The Historical Origins of Terrorism in America: 1644-1880.* New York: Routledge, 2014.

Lambert, Robert Stansbury. *South Carolina Loyalists in the American Revolution.* Columbia, SC: University of South Carolina Press, 1987.

Lancaster, Bruce, and J. H. Plumb. *The American Revolution.* Boston, MA: Houghton Mifflin, 2001.

Lenihan, Pádraig. *Consolidating Conquest: Ireland 1603-1727*. Harlow: Longman, 2008.

Leyburn, James. *The Scotch-Irish: A Social History*. Chapel Hill, NC: University of North Carolina Press, 1962.

Macrory, Patrick Arthur. *The Siege of Derry*. Oxford: Oxford University Press, 1988.

Maier, Pauline. *From Resistance to Revolution*. New York: Knopf, 1982.

McCarthy, Karen. *The Other Irish: Scots-Irish Rascals That Made America*. New York: Sterling, 2011.

McConnell, Michael N. *A Country Between: The Upper Ohio Valley and Its Peoples, 1724-1774*. Lincoln, NE: University of Nebraska Press, 1997.

McLuhan, Marshall, Quentin Fiore, and Jerome Agel. *The Medium Is the Message*. New York: Bantam Books, 1967.

Medley, Mary. *History of Anson County, North Carolina, 1750-1976*. Wadesboro, NC: Anson County Historical Society, 1976.

Meyer, Duane Gilbert. *The Highland Scots of North Carolina, 1732-1776*. Chapel Hill, NC: University of North Carolina Press, 1961.

Middleton, Richard. *Pontiac's War: It's Causes, Course, and Consequences*. New York: Routledge, 2007.

Miller, Kerby A. *Ireland and Irish America: Culture, Class, and Transatlantic Migration*. Dublin: Field Day in association with the Keough-Naughton Institute for Irish Studies at the University of Notre Dame, 2008.

Mitchell, Arthur. *South Carolina Irish*. Charleston, SC: History Press, 2011.

Myers, James P. *The Ordeal of Thomas Barton: Anglican Missionary in the Pennsylvania Backcountry, 1755-1780*. Bethlehem [PA]: Lehigh University Press, 2010.

Pennsylvania. *Colonial Records*. Philadelphia: J. Severns and Company, 1851.

Philyaw, Leslie. *Virginia's Western Visions: Political and Cultural Expansion on an Early American Frontier*. Knoxville, TN: University of Tennessee Press, 2004.

Pinn, Anthony. *Terror and Triumph: The Nature of Black Religion*. Minneapolis, MN: Fortress Press, 2003.

Polk, James, and Milo Milton Quaife. *The Diary of James K. Polk During His Presidency, 1845-1849*. Chicago, IL: McClurg, 1910.

Powell, William Samuel. *Dictionary of North Carolina Biography Vol. 6.* Chapel Hill, NC: University of North Carolina, 1996.

Rabushka, Alvin. *Taxation in Colonial America.* Princeton, NJ: Princeton University Press, 2009.

Reumann, John Henry Paul. *Muhlenberg's Ministerium, Ben Franklin's Deism, and the Churches of the Twenty-First Century: Reflections on the 250th Anniversary of the Oldest Lutheran Church Body in North America.* Grand Rapids, MI: W. B. Erdman's Publishing Company, 2011.

Revill, Janie. *A Compilation of the Original Lists of Protestant Immigrants to South Carolina, 1763-1773.* Baltimore, MD: Genealogical Publishing, 1974.

Rose, Nancy, and George Mendenhall Wilson. *George and Son: A Legacy of Letters.* Indianapolis, IN: Dog Ear Publishing, 2009.

Rupp, Daniel. *History of the Counties of Berks and Lebanon: Containing a Brief Account of the Indians.* Salem, MA: Higginson Book Company, 1992.

Scoggins, Michael C. *The Day It Rained Militia: Huck's Defeat and the Revolution in the South Carolina Backcountry, May-July 1780.* Charleston, SC: History Press, 2005.

Sellers, M. N. S. *American Republicanism: Roman Ideology in the United States Constitution.* New York: New York University Press, 1994.

Smith, Matthew. *A Declaration and Remonstrance of the Distressed and Bleeding Frontier Inhabitants of the Province of Pennsylvania.* Philadelphia: by W. Bradford, 1764.

Stockard, Sallie Walker. *The History of Guilford County, North Carolina.* Knoxville, TN: Gaut-Ogden, 1902.

Stone, William. *Life of Joseph Brant-Thayendanegea.* St. Clair Shores, MI: Scholarly Press, 1970.

Syfert, Scott. *The First American Declaration of Independence? The Disputed History of the Mecklenburg Declaration of May 20, 1775.* Jefferson, MO: McFarland and Company, 2013.

Taylor, Simon, and Marjorie Ogilvie Anderson. *Kings, Clerics, and Chronicles in Scotland, 500-1297.* Dublin, Ireland: Four Courts Press, 2000.

Taylor, W. C., and William Sampson. *History of Ireland.* New York: J and J Harper, 1833.

Tiedemann, Joseph. *Reluctant Revolutionaries: New York City and the Road to Independence, 1763-1776.* Ithaca, NY: Cornell University Press, 2008.

Trenchard, John, Thomas Gordon, and Ronald Hamowy. *Cato's Letters or Essays on Liberty, Civil and Religious, and Other Important Subjects.* Indianapolis, IN: Liberty Fund, 1995.

Troxler, Carole Watterson. *Farming Dissenters: The Regulator Movement in Piedmont North Carolina.* Raleigh, NC: Office of Archives and History, North Carolina Department of Cultural Resources, 2011.

Wallace, Helen Bruce. *Historic Paxton, Her Days and Her Ways, 1722-1913.* Harrisburg, PA: House of the Evangelical Church, 1913.

Waller, Maureen. *Ungrateful Daughters.* London: Hodder and Stoughton, 2002.

———. *Founding Political Warfare Documents of the United States.* Washington, DC: Crossbow Press, 2009.

Ward, Matthew C. *Breaking the Backcountry: The Seven Years' War in Virginia and Pennsylvania, 1754-1765.* Pittsburgh, PA: University of Pittsburgh Press, 2003.

Webb, James H. *Born Fighting: How the Scots-Irish Shaped America.* New York: Broadway Books, 2004.

Wilson, David. *United Irishmen, United States: Immigrant Radicals in the Early Republic.* Dublin: Four Courts Press, 1998.

Woodard, Colin. *American Nations: A History of the Eleven Rival Regional Cultures of North America.* New York: Viking, 2011.

Woodmason, Charles, and Richard James Hooker. *The Carolina Backcountry on the Eve of the Revolution; The Journal and Other Writings of Charles Woodmason, Anglican Itinerant.* Chapel Hill, NC: University of North Carolina Press, 1953.

Journal Articles

Adams, George. "The Carolina Regulators: A Note on Changing Interpretations." *The North Carolina Historical Review* 49, no. 4 (October 1972): 345-352.

Cavaioli, Frank J. "A Profile of the Paxton Boys: Murderers of the Conestoga Indians." *Journal of the Lancaster County Historical Society* 87, no. 3 (March 1983): 74-96.

Ekirch, Roger A. "'A New Government of Liberty': Hermon Husband's Vision of Backcountry North Carolina, 1755." *The William and Mary Quarterly* 34, no. 4 (October 1977): 632-646.

Griffin, Patrick. "The People with No Name: Ulster's Migrants and Identity Formation in Eighteenth-Century Pennsylvania." *The William and Mary Quarterly* 58, no. 3 (July 2001): 587-614.

Hindle, Brooke. "The March of the Paxton Boys." *The William and Mary Quarterly* 3, no. 4 (October 1946): 461-486.

Hudson, Arthur Palmer. "Songs of the North Carolina Regulators." *The William and Mary Quarterly* 4, no. 4 (October 1947): 470-485.

Klein, Rachel N. "Ordering the Backcountry: The South Carolina Regulation." *The William and Mary Quarterly* 38, no. 4 (October 1981): 661-680.

"Lists of Pennsylvania Settlers Murdered, Scalped and Taken Prisoners by Indians, 1755-1756." *The Pennsylvania Magazine of History and Biography* 32, no. 3 (1908): 309-319.

Maier, Pauline. "Popular Uprisings and Civil Authority in Eighteenth-Century America." *The William and Mary Quarterly* 27, no. 1 (January 1970): 3-35.

Piker, Joshua. "Colonists and Creeks: Rethinking the Pre-Revolutionary Southern Backcountry." *The Journal of Southern History* 70, no. 3 (August 2004): 503-540.

Sharpless, Isaac "Presbyterian and Quaker in Colonial Pennsylvania" *Journal of the Presbyterian Historical Society (1901-1930)* 3, no. 5 (March 1906):, 201-218.

Snydacker, Daniel. "Kinship and Community in Rural Pennsylvania, 1749-1820." *The Journal of Interdisciplinary History* 13, no. 1 (Summer 1982): 41-61.

Tiedemann, Joseph S. "Presbyterianism and the American Revolution in the Middle Colonies." *Church History* 74, no. 2 (June 2005): 306-344.

Whittenburg, James P. "Planters, Merchants, and Lawyers: Social Change and the Origins of the North Carolina Regulation." *The William and Mary Quarterly* 34, no. 2 (April 1977): 215-238.

Williamson, Hon. William. "Laws and Lawyers." *Quarterly Register and Journal of the American Education Society* 15, no. 1 (August 1843): 405-407.

Websites

Ancestry. "1781 Schedule" Pennsylvania, Northumberland County, Tax and Exoneration, 1768-1801. http://search.ancestry.com/search/db.aspx?dbid=2497&enc=1 (accessed 20 April 2014).

———. "1781 Tax List" New Jersey, Monmouth County, Census Substitutes Index, 1643-1890. http://search.ancestry.com/search/db.aspx?dbid=3562&enc=1 (accessed 20 April 2014).

Documenting the American South. "22 March 1768, Regulators' Advertisement No. 5 - Address from inhabitants near Haw River to the Orange County Vestry and General Assembly representatives." Colonial North Carolina Records. http://docsouth.unc.edu/csr/index.html/document/csr07-0264 (accessed 16 March 2014).

———. "Report by Charles Woodmason concerning religion in North Carolina, including a list of taxables." Colonial North Carolina Records. http://docsouth.unc.edu/csr/index.html/document/csr07-0152 (accessed 5 April 2014).

———. "Minutes of the Lower House of the North Carolina General Assembly." Colonial North Carolina Records. http://docsouth.unc.edu/csr/index.html/document/csr07-0156 (accessed 5 April 2014).

———. "Regulators' Advertisement No. 1 – Public notice concerning acts by public officials." Colonial North Carolina Records. http://docsouth.unc.edu/csr/index.html/document/csr07-0129 (accessed 5 April 2014)

Fold3. "Compiled Service Records of Soldiers Who Served in the American Army During the Revolutionary War." http://www.fold3.com/title_470/revolutionary_war_service_records/ (accessed 14 April 2014).

———. "Revolutionary War Pension and Bounty-Land Warrant Application Files." http://www.fold3.com/title_467/revolutionary_war_pensions/ (accessed 14 April 2014).

The Newberry Library. "North Carolina Historical Counties." http://historical-county.newberry.org/website/North_Carolina/viewer.htm (accessed 24 October 2013).

North Carolina History. "Petition of Reuben Searcy and Others and an Address to the People of Granville County." http://www.northcarolinahistory.org/encyclopedia/535/entry/ (accessed 9 March 2014).

South Carolina Department of Archives and History. "Williamson, Andrew, orders to John Caldwell, Advising him that a body of loyalists are marching on Augusta." Robert W. Gibbes Collection of Revolutionary War Manuscripts. http://www.archivesindex.sc.gov/onlinearchives/Thumbnails.aspx?recordId=174955 (accessed 22 April 2014).

Teaching American History. "Petition from Regulators of North Carolina. August 9th, 1769, General Readings on the Founding." http://teachingamericanhistory.org (accessed 23 November 2013).

University of Houston. "*To the INHABITANTS of the Province of North-Carolina.*" Digital-History; North Carolina Regulators. http://www.digitalhistory.uh.edu/disp_textbook.cfm?smtID=3&psid=3878 (accessed 4 April 2014).

Waymarking. "Carothers Family Marker." Tennessee Historical Markers. http://www.waymarking.com/waymarks/WMJHAZ_Carothers_Family_Franklin_TN (accessed 20 April 2014).

Newspapers

Harrisburg Patriot News. "Fighting Parson Carried the Good Book and a Rifle." Sunday, 22 February 1976.

Electronic Media

Oxford English Dictionary, 2d ed., s.v. "Regulators." Oxford: Oxford University Press, 1992. [CD-ROM].

Made in the USA
Lexington, KY
19 February 2017